As a qualified makeup artist Emily-Rose works throughout fashion, commercial, television and the wedding industry. She has been the makeup artist for many music artists including Tinie Tempah and the Backstreet Boys, and has worked with the BBC and Channel S (Sky 814) Television's version of *The X Factor*. Emily is passionate about makeup and loves to make someone feel confident and beautiful. She has been the make-up artist for many stars at red carpet events. Alongside her regular work, Emily has also launched a makeup therapy service supporting all illness, disabilities and the elderly and has recently launched her own range of nutritious lipstick. To find out more, visit her website: www.emilyrosemakeupartist.co.uk

Also by Emily-Rose

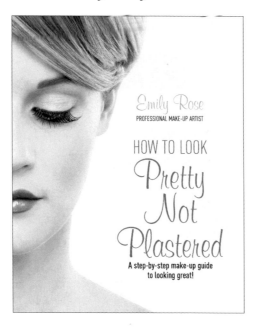

How to
Look Beautiful
Forever

EMILY-ROSE

Constable & Robinson Ltd.
55–56 Russell Square
London WC1B 4HP
www.constablerobinson.com

First published in the UK by How To Books,
an imprint of Constable & Robinson Ltd., 2014

A copy of the British Library Cataloguing in Publication
Data is available from the British Library

ISBN 978-1-84528-495-4 (trade paperback)
ISBN 978-1-47211-011-4 (ebook)

Printed and bound in the China

3 5 7 9 10 8 6 4 2

Contents

vii

Acknowledgements

This book has become very special, as so many people have been involved in creating it; family, friends, colleagues and strangers alike. As I wrote it, I not only wanted to provide my readers with a guide book to makeup, but also to help people to achieve a greater level of confidence, love and self-esteem. Over the two-year period of putting together *How to Look Beautiful Forever*, I went through some very difficult times both, medically and emotionally, an experience which reinforced how important it is to have love for yourself and others. I hope my own challenges will have enabled me to create words that will resonate with my readers. During the time of writing I also fell pregnant with my second daughter, who was born in January 2013; my two beautiful daughters, Lara and Megan, light up my life every single day. Seeing them grow and develop fascinates and inspires me continuously.

My family have been simply spectacular, during tough times they backed me solidly, urging me on to complete my goal.

My husband Anton is a wonderful man, full of love, generosity, kindness and a heart that just keeps on giving. His support and love for me has been indescribable, his contribution in helping me to bring this book together invaluable not only in ideas, but in every other way that one person could help and care for another.

My parents (Christine and Nic) have an immeasurable amount of time, patience and love for their children. Hours have been spent supporting me in ways that have allowed me to complete my book and regain full recovery.

Thank you to my sisters, Jess and Kate; you always make me smile and giggle. Thank you for your input on image content and for your overall sisterly love.

To my friends, your guidance, your faith and your loving support has injected strength into my life and left me feeling incredibly touched.

To my publishers, your patience and understanding could not go un-noted; you really have been an amazing team to work with.

Thank you to my lovely friend Jordan (Portal PR). You have encouraged me every step of the way.

To Kate McIntyre, thank you for being my cover girl! Thank you to Semone Hairstylist for being part of the front cover and to Richard Grebby Photography for shooting it.

Thank you to Jessica De Mattos Photography, your hard work and dedication to this project has been out of this world. My thanks also to John Burgess of Waterham Photographic Studios for all of your input; Samantha Jones, for the fun we had on our Olympic-style photo shoot; Ben Anker Photography for the beautiful image of Thandie; Will Sterling and the crew at *Denim Magazine* and to Matt Bristow (Rubber Duck Does Photography). A huge thank you also to session stylists Natalie Shirlaw, Vicki Lord and all my models, all of you have been incredible.

Every single person in my life has had something to do with making the possibility of this book a reality. Thank you, everyone x

Introduction

Previously I wrote a makeup book called *How to Look Pretty Not Plastered* – a beginners guide, for teenagers. This book, *How to Look Beautiful Forever*, aims to inspire women of all ages to enjoy the magical world of makeup, whether you are 20 or 70+. I aim to show you how you can recreate new looks for yourself, and look beautiful forever. Whether you are a mum, a nan, a career woman, or a girl who just loves makeup, this book will teach you the skills to care for your skin and wear the look you want to wear from youth to maturity.

The correct makeup creates a youthful appearance no matter what age you are, and the aim of my book is to teach you how to do it with a positive approach. My focus is upon feeling confident in being who you are, and emphasising that life's aim does not need to be to look forever young. The focus in the media and advertising seems to be on anti-ageing products, so it's no wonder that so many people feel a sense of anxiety about growing older.

The fact is, beauty is as much about the mind as it is about the body. By focusing on what we dislike, or how we don't want to look, all we do is create more things that we decide that we want to change, or wish away. The trick is to start focusing on what you love, start to notice your features and fall in love with them.

Be comfortable and confident with whom you are, no matter what stage of life you are at – that is what being beautiful really means.

Digital editing

As you are probably all aware, the digital manipulation of photographs is ubiquitous in the media world, and often the images you see in print, such as those in high-fashion magazines and makeup books, have been digitally edited. Even the ones that 'appear' non-edited have often been changed in one way or another. Throughout this book, you will see step-by-step thumbnails of makeup being applied. These are 'raw', 'unedited' so that you can see how makeup truly looks, even when applied by a professional makeup artist. They are followed by a final image, which will have been edited and is provided for inspiration. By doing this I hope to cater both for reality, and for our creative minds.

1

I also want to do this in order to show you that you are as capable of applying makeup to a professional standard as a makeup artist is. Even we, when applying eyeshadow, tackle the issue of fallout beneath the eyes, and with each image, I will guide you through tips and tricks towards achieving a flawless finish.

Too many women feel that they are 'no good at applying makeup' because they look at a digitally-edited image for inspiration and become frustrated if they can't achieve that 'perfect finish'. They may not always realise that could they see the image before editing, they would find the look somewhat more achievable.

I will be using women from all walks of life, both models and non-models, of all ages within this book to emphasise just how beautiful you all are. It is amazing how makeup can transform every person in the world. Women who aren't models hold their own against the models in my book. That's because they are all just real women.

Keeping it simple

Simple, well-moisturised makeup is the easiest way to maintain youthful looks. Keeping eyeliner classic and skin soft and radiant creates a timeless effect. It doesn't matter if it's historical makeup we're interested in or the latest catwalk looks, everything can be given an elegant, modern twist and made appropriate for you – similar to the way that high-street clothing brands take inspiration from the current catwalk trends and launch a more subtle version for the everyday consumer.

I'm a strong believer that we can wear any look that we like, by taking elements of that look and enhancing or taming it to suit our individual style, features, skin tone and age.

Modern makeup is designed to look real. By real, I mean that we accentuate our features, so that we look at our most beautiful, rather than plastering it on so that all that we see is our makeup. Makeup has wonderful power to make us appear healthy, even if we are poorly, to help us look youthful, no matter what our age, to depict a story or our personality. Keeping makeup simple draws attention to key features. I once heard a stylist say that keeping fashion simple is beautiful, it makes a statement – I like to apply this theory to makeup. This of course is just my opinion and not a set-in-stone rule.

Makeup has changed dramatically over the decades. Long gone are the powdery, one-dimensional foundations. Today's foundations illuminate, reflect light to minimise wrinkles and generally create a three-dimensional appearance. In the past heavy contouring (shading) had to be used, much like theatre makeup, in order to create this effect. Now, with foundation being manufactured in such a way that it looks and feels like our real skin, you can sculpt your face with a minimum amount of product.

With today's products mature skin really can flourish! Years ago when makeup was heavy, flat and matte, mature women struggled to apply it as their skin became less elastic. Now, makeup is full of moisture, plumping the skin and creating a flawless, radiant, healthy finish – in fact, mature women can almost certainly guarantee that a little makeup will most definitely enhance their beauty, rather than worrying that it will accentuate their age. The queries that I am most often faced with are: 'how do I apply it?'; 'makeup has changed so much, I don't know what suits me anymore'; or 'how do all of these different products work?' There are some simple tricks that work from youth to maturity so let's get started!

3

CHAPTER 1

Shopping for Makeup

Women often tell me how confused they get with all of the products available. Which ones should I buy? Should I wear all of them at the same time? It seems like such a lot of makeup to pile onto my skin, surely I'll end up looking like I'm wearing a mask?

It may seem overwhelming – many products can be used to create a look, but often only small amounts are needed, and you only need to use the ones which will benefit the look you want to create. Also, you may think you need to go through the same steps with every look, but you don't. For example, one look may be amazing with contoured cheekbones, whilst another might be better with clean, fresh and rosy cheeks, using only blusher. Plus, depending on how you apply it, blusher, or bronzer, used alone can produce the same effect as shading does, giving you contoured cheekbones.

Yes, there are many products to choose from – there are some that you cannot live without and others that are a special treat. I'll take you through what I feel is beneficial for each look, but ultimately there are no solid rules to makeup, purely guidelines for achieving a flawless finish. Makeup should capture your own individuality, so feel free with it and have fun. The key point is that you don't have to use all of your products at the same time for every single look, and if you remember that 'less is more' you will never look like you are wearing a mask.

It's a common misconception that makeup counter staff will sell you the right products every time. In fact, hundreds of my clients have been miss-sold products for the sake of sales, or sold the wrong colour foundation because of a lack of knowledge. Get savvy yourself so that you can identify your own shades and needs, and feel confident in asking staff about their latest products and whether they will be of benefit to you. Achieving beautiful makeup doesn't necessarily mean using the products with the highest price tag, either.

Choose products that suit you and that you feel great in. Most counters will provide testers, particularly for foundation, so don't be afraid to ask for one. I urge you to try before you buy to ensure that the product that you are purchasing wears well on your skin throughout the day and is the correct shade for you. Having a makeover from one of the artists at a counter is a good way to try before you buy – don't be afraid to tell them what you like and how you like to wear it as they apply it, it will help them to identify the right products for you. At the end of the makeover don't feel pressured to buy anything; there is no obligation to do so unless you want to.

You can gain a rough idea about how your makeup might look when it's applied by a makeup artist at a cosmetic counter from the way their own makeup looks. Use this as your guide for approaching the right person for you.

Makeup hygiene

I cannot emphasise how important makeup hygiene is. Often, sensitive skin may not be as sensitive as we think, but rather makeup has not been carefully nurtured, or perhaps it has aged. That's not to say that ingredients don't play a part in triggering a reaction in sensitive skin, but by carefully looking after your makeup you will guarantee not only lovely makeup application but also avoid spreading bacteria onto your skin, and prevent your makeup from degrading in quality.

People remember to sanitise their hands, makeup brushes and surfaces, but do you remember to sanitise your makeup – the very product that comes into contact with your eyes, skin and lips and that can allow bacteria to enter the body? Have you ever had a compact powder for so long that the surface appears shiny and hard in patches? That is a build-up of oil from your skin embedded in the makeup where a brush or powder puff has been used again and again over the product, without cleansing the makeup or the brush between each application. Daily use of a product such as Cosmetic Sanitizer Mist on new makeup will remove bacteria and keep your products looking new. This is specifically designed to gently clean the makeup itself and is also designed to be non-abrasive so that it will not degrade the quality of the product.

For makeup artists, it is absolutely essential to cleanse makeup between clients; this will prevent spreading infection from one person to the next and contaminating your makeup.

Below, I have detailed makeup hygiene tips, followed by a description of the shelf life of different makeup products. For best results always discard old products and replace with fresh new ones within the recommended time frame.

- Avoid sharing mascara with friends to avoid any possibility of passing around eye infections – if you do share, it is best to use a separate mascara wand, or a disposable mascara wand, and avoid double dipping. Use a new wand for each new application, even if that means two per eye!

- Avoid where possible double-dipping into any makeup product. Clean your brush between each dip, or use a spatula, cotton bud or the end of your brush to scrape a small amount of product out of the pot onto the back of your hand or onto a mixing palette. (Tip – a small piece of Perspex makes a fabulous mixing palette.)

- Sharpen pencils (lip liners and eyeliners) between each use to remove bacteria. If you use a twist-up pencil, roll it onto a tissue sprayed with brush cleanser between each use.

Makeup shelf life

Mascara: three to six months
Eye pencils: twelve to eighteen months
Eyeshadow: two years
Eye cream: six months
Liquid, cream and gel foundation: two years
Concealer: two years
Powder: two years
Powder blusher: two years
Cream blusher: two years
Lipstick: twelve to eighteen months
Sunscreen: two years
Face cream: two years

Beautiful brushes

Whether you are a professional makeup artist, a beginner or a frequent user of makeup, your brushes and your fingers are your best friends. However, if it's that flawless airbrushed look you are after, brushes really are the way forward.

That said, I never use brushes or fingers alone – I use both. For example, I use a fluffy brush to apply foundation, then use my fingers to really warm the product into the skin, allowing the product to become flawless and eliminating tell-tale brush stroke lines. If I use my fingers to apply foundation, I use a fine-tipped concealer brush to cover blemishes.

Whether you are working with foundation, cream eyeshadow or cream blusher, your fingers warm the product, allowing it to glide onto your skin and give you 100 per cent control. If you are using a foundation brush, warm the product on the back of your hand first. Use your hand as if it were a palette.

A fluffy foundation brush – the new revolution in foundation brushes, I find that this gives a much more flawless application than a flat brush.

A bronzer/blusher brush.

A powder brush.

A fluffy eyeshadow brush – great for blending.

Flat eyeshadow brush – great for pressing eyeshadow onto the eyelid.

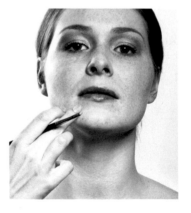

Small eyeshadow brush – great for detail.

Eyebrow brush – angled for a precise and clean shape.

Concealer brushes – large for bigger areas and tiny for pinpoint concealing over spots and small blemishes.

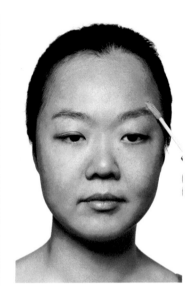

A fine angled eyeliner brush. A flat push liner brush. A dry mascara wand/eyebrow comb.

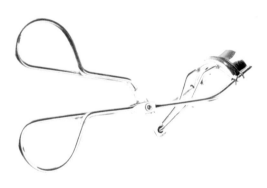

Eyelash curlers. Lip brush.

I tend to recommend that you should avoid buying brushes purely on price. Sometimes the quality of a cheaper brush can be similar to that of a more expensive brush, but one is retailed at a higher price because of the brand. Have you ever bought a really expensive top, only to walk into the cheaper shop round the corner to find a similar one that's half the price but the look and quality is pretty much the same?

This is not to say that I recommend that you buy cheap brushes. Many of the amazing brushes on the market are the more expensive ones, mainly because of the material that they are made from – especially if they are real hair – however I'll never forget the day that I walked in to Charles Fox, only to find that the brushes were fantastic quality, and literally

a third of the price of the previous brand of brushes I had been using, I now tend to use a mixture of real and synthetic bristle brushes. The quality of synthetic bristle brushes is becoming so good, that there is little difference between the two.

How do you know which brushes to buy? Test them for feel and durability. Sweep the brush over the back of your hand; if the bristles feel too shiny and slippery, you may find it difficult to apply makeup quickly with them, as there is often not enough density within the bristles to grab and hold onto the pigment of the product that you are using. If the bristles feel too coarse, you may find them difficult to blend with. The perfect density is in-between both of these textures – fluffy, soft but dense.

If you stand the brush on the tip of its bristles on the back of your hand, you will be able to see if they are dense enough – if the bristles collapse completely the likelihood is that they are too soft, if they feel rough and pokey they are too coarse, if they stand nicely and gently on the back of your hand it should be a great brush.

Lastly, test the durability of the brush by tugging the bristles very gently. If any bristles fall out, the brush may fall apart quickly and probably isn't worth the investment. If the bristles stand strong its durability should be great – so long as you care for it.

If you opt for brushes with a pointed tip, this will give you complete control and greater accuracy when you are adding detail.

Once you have purchased your brushes, look after them: they are your magic tools! Use a cotton pad and brush cleanser to cleanse the bristles after every use (this will fight against bacteria build-up and will also prolong the life of your brush, as leaving product on a brush can cause it to deteriorate). Once every one to two weeks deep cleanse your brushes to remove anything deep within the bristles. Pop a small amount of gentle baby shampoo or brush cleanser into the palm of your hand, swirl the brush through it and massage the bristles, then rinse them off thoroughly under running lukewarm water. Avoid soaking the brushes as this may cause the glue to dissolve and the brush to fall apart. Roll the brushes in a towel to soak off excess water and then lay them on a table to dry. Never lay the bristles down directly on the table to dry, always leave the bristles hanging over the edge of a surface like a table – this will allow them to dry in perfect shape and will prevent them from becoming damp and smelly.

When your brushes start to moult or collapse then you will know it's time to replace them.

CHAPTER 2

The Foundation of Beautiful Makeup

Looking after our health and our skin

Looking after our general health and skin is where beautiful makeup all begins. Inner and outer beauty needs to work in harmony and to achieve this we need to look after our bodies too. What we eat and drink, how much exercise we do, and how we sleep, relax, and have fun all make a difference to how we feel and look.

It's really simple: if we want to look and feel radiant and healthy, we need to lead a radiant and healthy lifestyle. It's not really rocket science, or anything we don't already know – health campaigns fill every magazine, TV screen and billboard we see these days.

Understanding why it is so important to look after your skin is the first step to health, well-being, being beautiful and applying beautiful makeup.

Our skin

Our skin is the largest organ of the body.

- It is what allows us to synthesise vitamin D when exposed to sunlight (vital for our health).

- It protects the body from harmful UV rays.

- It stops water getting in and out of the body – a type of waterproofing.

- It helps to regulate body temperature.

- It grows continuously.

- It stops poisonous chemicals and germs from getting into the body.

- It contains sense organs that enable us to feel any changes in the environment, such as heat, cold, wet, dry.

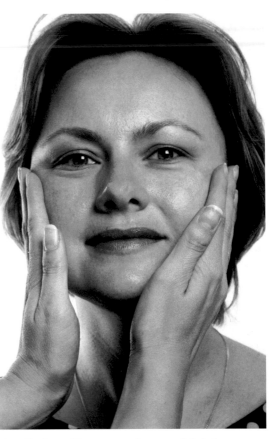

Our skin changes throughout our lives. As a baby we have what is called 'normal' skin, with no enlarged pores, no blemishes or breakouts of spots, just absolutely perfectly smooth, even-toned skin.

When we become teenagers our skin begins to change as we go through puberty, and hormones can play havoc with our skin. It is still extremely youthful but very temperamental!

Later, as our skin moves into the young adult phase, it can start to settle down and breakouts may ease a little, although this really varies from person to person.

From the age of twenty-five our skin begins to change again – it starts to mature. People notice these changes at different times; some people are lucky enough to keep their youthful skin for many years, whilst others age more rapidly. There are all sorts of factors involved in the ageing process.

Understanding the ageing process

As we get older fine lines and wrinkles appear – but these give your face character! If you study the face of anyone who has had Botox treatment, you'll notice that often, especially if it has been over used, the face has lost much of its character. For example, the person can't move their forehead, or mouth in the same way as someone without any intervention can. This limits the amount of personality that can shine though, the inner beauty that can light up a face no matter how old it is.

Women pass through phases of beauty, and the women who often look most beautiful are those who embrace ageing and adapt their makeup to enhance each phase.

What is more ageing than a few lines and wrinkles however is dull skin, which is why cleansing is so important, and we will come to that on page 18.

What to do with a lacklustre complexion

If your skin looks dull or tired you should exfoliate and use an uplifting mask. Massage your face with facial oil or moisturiser to boost circulation. Apply an illuminating primer to your skin prior to foundation. Use a light-reflective or dewy/sheeny finish foundation. For that naturally glossy glow, use cream blush instead of powder. Highlight the high points of your face to add brightness using a cream product. Drink plenty of water, get some good sleep and go for a walk to get your circulation pumping. I also find eating avocado and nuts rich in healthy oil can give skin a real boost.

The two types of ageing

There are two types of ageing:

- **Intrinsic ageing**, which is the process that we inherit through our genes, and is therefore pretty much out of our control.

- **Extrinsic ageing**, which is how we care for our health and our skin.

We do have some control over extrinsic ageing. For example, if we smoke, sunbathe frequently, drink too much alcohol, take recreational drugs, eat unhealthy food on a regular basis or neglect our skin, we are at greater risk of increasing, or accelerating the ageing process. However, if we nourish and take care of our bodies, both internally and externally, we may well help ourselves to prolong our youthful looks.

Teen years: thirteen to twenty

When we are young our skin is full of moisture and elasticity – if you were to gently pull the skin, it would ping straight back into place again. The middle layer of the skin (the dermis), has elastin fibres which help to prevent the skin from sagging, and protein called collagen which helps to keep the skin plump and prevents it from wrinkling, thus giving it a youthful appearance.

As puberty kicks in hormones can become unbalanced, causing the sebaceous glands to produce more sebum. This can result in congested skin such as blackheads. High progesterone levels can lead to acne, which is very common throughout puberty.

Poor diet, smoking, alcohol, recreational drugs and lack of sleep can all play their part in increasing problematic skin, but at this age the skin can recover quickly. The older we get, the slower the cell renewal becomes, until eventually it stops altogether. So, if you look after your skin now, you may find it much easier to maintain beautiful skin as you age.

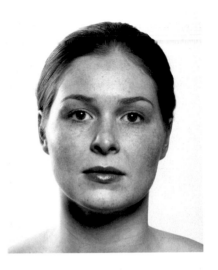

Twenty to thirty years

Hormones begin to settle down at this age, and so skin is at its prime. It looks radiant, glowing and youthful. There are little or no lines developing and the facial structure is strong.

Thirty to forty years

The skin's reproduction begins to slow down now and often the skin starts to become drier. Fine lines often appear around the neck area first. The facial tissues begin to lose their fatty layer and under eyes can begin to look tired. Elasticity is lessened, so skin doesn't ping back as quickly as it once did. Using preventative products such as sun cream, moisturiser and also drinking plenty of water and having a good diet will help you to maintain youthful looks.

Always remember that your neck and hands will reflect your age, so it is vital that you keep these areas well hydrated with moisturiser. The jawline is still strong at this stage but may begin to lose some definition towards the latter years.

Forty to fifty years

During this decade features are still clearly defined. Fine lines and sometimes slightly deeper wrinkles may

become more permanent. At this stage of your life the elastin fibres and collagen, which support the skin, begin to diminish.

The skin starts to become thinner, which means that it may be more prone to sun damage, blemishes, broken capillaries and pigmentation (age spots).

Fifty to seventy years

Menopause will have begun within this age group and the skin will be much more loose and thin. Eyes may become puffy and the muscles around the eyes develop depressions, which we know as wrinkles.

The lip line becomes less defined. The sebaceous glands slow down and therefore the skin is more prone to infection. Some women may find that they begin to develop facial hair, particularly around the mouth and chin; this is because testosterone is not being balanced by oestrogen.

Skin may feel coarser in texture.

Seventy years+

By the time you reach this age, skin has the appearance of being soft. Deeper creases run from the outer corners of the mouth and from the nose towards the lips. Skin may appear paper-thin in areas such as the neck, chest and hands. This is because with such a lack of sebum being produced there is no longer much hydration within the skin – this is a crucial time to add it back by using hydrating creams, facial oils and moisturising cleansers.

The face may appear to droop now, as there is very little fat to support the facial structure anymore. You may also notice pigmentation marks appearing (areas of darkened skin), particularly on the arms and hands.

How to prevent premature ageing

Although our genes largely determine our life span, including the rate of our ageing process, there is much you can do to slow down the ravages of time. This primarily involves maintaining a healthy lifestyle – eating well, sleeping well, staying safe in the sun

– as well as remaining mentally active, as the longer your brain is active the longer you will remain alert.

Moisturising your skin to avoid premature ageing

Think moisture, moisture, and moisture! This is the most essential element in caring for your skin as it ages. You can help to prevent your skin from ageing too quickly by feeding its elasticity. When pregnant women try to avoid stretch marks by ensuring that the skin on their tummy is well hydrated, it is the same kind of rule that applies to the skin on your face.

The best protection from the sun is to cover up by wearing a hat that shades your face. If you are going to expose your skin directly to the sun be liberal with your sun cream, as it will help to prevent the signs of rapid ageing, such as leather-like skin and age spots (brown pigmentation marks).

When cleansing and moisturising your skin always use circular upward motions – this acts against the force of gravity, which as we age naturally forces skin to droop. Cleanse using gentle, nourishing, moisturising products which help to maintain the skin's pH balance.

Focus on caring for your neck; it is one area of our bodies that can age rather quickly and reveals the tell-tale signs of ageing. Keeping it well moisturised and protected from the sun will help to reduce this.

Never drag your skin or rub too hard, the skin becomes thinner as we age and you may risk damaging it or causing it to age more rapidly, particularly around the eye area, which is a thin area of skin at any age.

Caring for your skin

I believe that skin doesn't necessarily have a 'type', but that there are different categories that our skin falls in and out of depending on how it is reacting to the environment, our lifestyle and our hormones. It is important to assess your skin on a daily basis, and to re-evaluate your skincare routine. Some days it may need a little more TLC!

Skin conditions

If you have a skin condition you should seek advice from your dermatologist.

Be aware of ingredients that irritate you, keep note of them.

Avoid perfumed products and be sure to research ingredients before putting them on to your skin.

Identifying the skin categories

Skin basically falls into these general categories:

Dry. Winter weather, harsh soap, ageing, products that you may be sensitive to, and your health can all play a big part in why you may be suffering from dry skin. If your skin feels or looks dry, feed it with extra-rich moisture. After cleansing, massage a facial oil or moisturiser into your skin, and apply additional product to the areas that feel drier – if it is a similar consistency all over, you can use a double layer.

Oily. Oily skin can leave your makeup slipping and sliding; you will see a sheen glistening over the skin. If you blot your face with a tissue, you may see the excess oil transfer onto it. Oily skin occurs when the sebaceous glands are over-active and produce excess oil, which can lead to congested skin.

Keep oily skin hydrated using lightweight products. Myth has it that oily skin types should avoid oil because it may block the pores. But in fact oil-based products have the opposite effect on oily skin. If you add oil to water it separates, and our skin reacts in much the same way. So oily skin sits with oily products much more comfortably. This goes for foundations and other oil-based products too! Steer clear of foaming cleansers that contain sodium lauryl sulphate: this can strip your skin of too much natural oil and cause your glands to produce even more to compensate for rapid dehydration.

Combination. Combination skin is often dry in places and oily through the T-zone. Using gentle cleanser and a pH balancing toner is good for re-balancing. Use moisturiser or facial oil as you would normally, and add extra hydration to your drier areas.

Sensitive. Sensitive skin is often confused with sensitised skin. Skin can become sensitised by an irritant within a particular product, and it can also settle back down again. Steering away from perfumed products and products containing harsh chemicals is usually the key to keeping reactions at bay.

Cleansing your skin

So many women I meet tell me that they don't cleanse, or at least just use a baby wipe to remove their makeup. Makeup formulas are so long-wearing these days, that if you don't cleanse it off thoroughly it can remain on the skin, and a build-up of old makeup would be pretty challenging for your poor pores! Having said that, I'm a firm believer in not over-cleansing. Over-cleansing can result in stripping away the natural oils within your skin. Cleansing is also, from my point of view, the most important part of makeup application, because much like an artist it creates a smooth canvas for you to work on. For example, if you find your foundation clinging in patches to your skin, or looking dry and cakey on the surface, the likelihood is that you have a build-up of dead skin cells. These need to be gently exfoliated away and the new skin hydrated. If your skin is maintained deliciously, your makeup will look delicious too!

    I advise using a gel cleanser because it produces less foam. The more foam a cleanser produces generally the more natural oil it can strip from your skin, thus causing the skin to produce more oil in compensation and in a fight to keep your skin hydrated. I recommend double cleansing, once to remove the dirt and a second time to really give your skin a deep clean.

Toning your skin

Toning re-balances the pH of the skin (a poor pH balance has been linked to spots and wrinkles) and also refreshes it, so long as the toner you choose is not astringent. Aggressive toners can strip the acid mantle (the slightly acidic film on the surface of the skin acting as a barrier to bacteria, viruses and contaminants) leading to oiliness. The natural pH of our skin should be around 5.5. If too much oil is stripped from the skin and it becomes more alkaline, say pH 6 or 7, it may begin to break the barrier down, which can allow bacteria into the skin and moisture to escape. With a perfectly balanced pH, skin retains optimum moisture, is protected, and you will have helped to prevent premature ageing. It is good to use a toner after cleansing, or after using a mask. Toner can also help to shrink the appearance of pores. Either spritz toner lightly over the face after cleansing, or apply it to the skin using a damp cotton wool pad. Remember to choose lovely gentle toners.

Exfoliating your skin

Exfoliate your skin with a product that is super-soft and gentle. The skin on our face is delicate, therefore it's important not to tug it around too much, so work the product into your skin using gentle circular motions with your fingers.

If you have mature skin exfoliation is particularly important because as the skin ages it becomes thinner and is more prone to damage. Peeling exfoliating products are lovely – they come in either jelly or cream form, you massage them into the skin in circular motions and as you do so the dead skin cells and grime from the environment literally peel off! These are very gentle because you do not feel harsh grains.

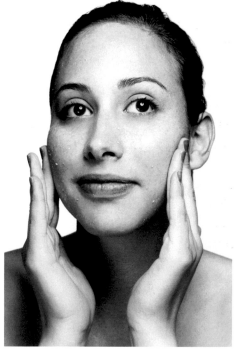

Using face masks

Face masks are brilliant if you need an instant pick-me-up, especially if it's the morning after an alcohol-fuelled night when skin can be left feeling dehydrated and tired. Opt for a mask that is hydrating (to hydrate), clarifying (to draw out impurities) or anti-inflammatory (soothing – great for redness in the skin).

Moisturising

It is an inescapable fact that every single skin type needs moisturiser.

Some days we may need more moisture, other days slightly less. Even if you suffer from oily skin, starving it of moisture could actually increase the sebum produced beneath your skin, causing even oilier skin and congestion within your pores.

Our skin is the most active at night – it is when cell renewal happens – so this is a vital time to apply a rich, hydrating, nourishing moisturiser.

In the morning, before you put your makeup on, it is best to use a lightweight product, which will keep oils balanced. This also helps to give a smooth and longer-lasting base; our skin will absorb lightweight formulas, allowing makeup to sit perfectly on top without slipping and sliding.

With heavy formulas, skin tends to absorb what it needs and the rest may just sit on the surface. As a result any other product you put on top of this will melt away. Avoid applying moisturiser directly to your under-eye area: the skin here is thin and therefore often cannot absorb all of it, which can cause puffy eyes.

Facial oil

Although it is widely thought that using oil on your face is only something that you would do if your skin were very dry, this couldn't be further from the truth. The lightweight consistency allows the product to be easily absorbed into the skin, immediately moisturising, softening and conditioning it.

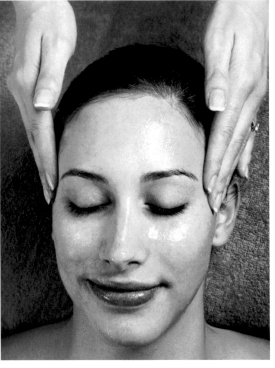

Massaging facial oil into your skin after cleansing at night instead of using a moisturiser both hydrates and tones the face. Using pre-cleanse oil is also great for removing surface dirt before you apply your regular cleanser.

Massaging botanical oils into the skin can help to boost circulation and plump out fine lines.

Eye cream

Even if you are twenty there is no reason why you can't use eye cream. In fact, I actively promote it. It's really easy to look at our skin as a teenager and think, 'My skin is great, it's young, I don't need to do much'. Wrong. This is the stage where your skin has so much elasticity, it zaps up moisture and glows all year round. If you can get into the swing of nourishing it now, the elasticity is more likely to stay with you throughout the years.

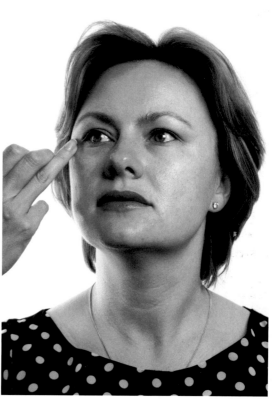

The skin beneath our eyes is thin and so is likely to age much more quickly due to the effects of everyday life: the weather, alcohol, smoking, late nights, busy lifestyle, etc.

Pop eye cream along the top of your cheekbone to keep your eyes cared for. The skin absorbs the moisture upwards, drawing the amount it needs to beneath your eyes. At night, apply the eye cream further along your cheekbone following the socket line up to your brow bone and down to the bridge of your nose (forming a circle around the eye). This will act as a mask for the eyes whilst you sleep.

Top tips for a healthy complexion

Beauty sleep

Beauty sleep is essential. It's not just about looking good, it's about feeling great! Just as babies need x amount of sleep to grow, we need x amount of sleep to function healthily. Sleep is an essential time for your body, and for the repair and regeneration of skin cells and tissues, which we shed on a daily basis.

A lack of sleep causes all of our bodily functions to slow down, affecting us both physically and mentally. It can make you feel run down, low and reduce your energy levels.

If you find your busy lifestyle's taking over ...

Take a sheet of paper and map out your day, organising your commitments according to their priority. You may be pleasantly surprised and find that there are some things on your list that aren't as essential as exercise or sunshine, for example. It's really easy in life to make excuses which allow us not to do the things that we think are going to be tough, especially if we feel tired, but the fact is, these activities rejuvenate us and actually improve our work/pleasure balance of life. Using this technique you will soon be prioritising your day the right way.

You need to allow yourself time to relax and unwind, enabling you to sleep soundly. It sounds silly but head back to childhood and give yourself a bedtime routine. You'll be amazed how you begin to stick to it, and how your body clock changes to fit with it.

Diet

This subject drives me crazy. Every time we pick up a magazine there is a new weird and wonderful diet in there, usually accredited to a celebrity just to entice us a little bit more. Is this really the diet of that particular celebrity? Who knows!

If you are a woman who is guilty of yo-yo dieting, or diet hopping, give yourself a break. You are beautiful just the way that you are. Slow down, balance your life and allow yourself to eat what your body asks for in moderation. I'm not talking about those little cravings that tell you 'I must eat five bars of chocolate', I'm talking about allowing yourself that piece of chocolate and balancing it with an equal amount of healthy food such as fruit, veg, salad, lean meat, fish, nuts, or seeds whilst maintaining a healthy level of exercise.

Youthful skin starts from within

The fact is, as the old saying goes 'we are what we eat', and beauty really does begin from within.

A variety of foods provide essential vitamins and minerals that are required to keep the body working at its most efficient level. These foods hydrate the skin, replace cells and maintain general growth and repair. They also provide powerful antioxidants to the body.

Amino acids are known as the building blocks of life. They are essential in stimulating the growth and repair of our skin cells, and are critical in maintaining our skin's moisture barrier. Amino acids also make up the neurotransmitters within our brains, which produce our happy, balancing chemicals (and aid our mental well-being).

Essential amino acids are obtained from the protein within certain foods that we consume. Amino acids are used in every cell of our bodies to build the proteins that we need to survive. A rainbow of fruit and veg help to give our skin a healthy glow; they also help to hydrate, heal and protect our skin from things like sun damage and environmental damage. Foods that contain beta-carotene can even help to restore collagen! Here are a few examples of foods that can give us a real boost: Fish, chicken, turkey, beef, dairy, eggs and a variety of fruit and veg such as melon, strawberries, blueberries, raspberries, apples, oranges, kiwi, grapefruit, mangos, pomegranates, cherries, cucumber, lettuce, spinach, alfalfa, beetroot, celery, carrots, turnips, green pepper, mint, bok choy (or pak choi), broccoli and mushrooms.

If you are a lover of sugar, caffeine and carbs, try cutting down on the refined products (white sugar, bread, pasta, rice and most processed foods). They contain very little nutritional value and may also in some cases act as a depressant. Instead switch to the more nutritional wholemeal varieties of pasta, rice, bread etc. The effects that refined sugars have on the body are still unknown to lots of people. Just last week I was talking with my friend about sugar, and a girl nearby turned to me and asked, 'What's wrong with sugar, then. What does it do?' Considering how much of the stuff is packed into food and drink these days, it's scary to think how little people understand about it.

Be aware of misleading marketing tricks when you are shopping. The cereal bar you've just picked up to replace the choccy bar in your right hand, enticed by the promise that it is better for you, may not be any better for you at all. Some of these so-called healthy snacks contain just as much sugar as the sweet refined ones! Always study the back of the packaging for nutritional value – you are looking for sugar content in particular.

I'll never forget the time when I picked up a bottle of healthy smoothie, and flipped it over to check the ingredients, only to discover a whopping 19 grams of sugar in one bottle! I quickly put it down and grabbed a bottle of water!

Raw foods are a fantastic substitute for sweet foods. You know you've hit a healthy jackpot when you see a product description like this:

Raw fruit & nut whole food

100% natural ingredients!
1 of 5 a day
No added sugar or syrups
Cold pressed
Never baked
Guilt-free goodness

And don't be fooled by the word 'diet' – diet foods often contain more artificial toxins than the full fat versions.

For the sake of keeping my integrity intact – yes, I still indulge from time to time in sugary things and all things 'nice', but I try to balance it out with the good stuff.

Exercise

Regular exercise gets the blood pumping around our bodies. It increases the heart rate and allows the lungs to have a workout too. The stimulation of blood flow shows within the skin and makes you look radiant.

Exercise is proven to reduce stress levels and also to keep a healthy immune system and is essential, even if it's just a stroll in the park to boost your vitamin D levels.

Fit exercise into your working day ...

If you tend to see exercise only as going to the gym, going swimming or doing some form of sport, please allow yourself to think outside of the box. Exercise is exercise even if it means walking or riding your bike to work.

Nipping out on your break for a stroll around the park, or heading out for a dance after work is *exercise*. Exercise is simply about allowing your body to move and your heart rate to rise for at least twenty minutes per day. If you can exercise for more than twenty minutes, then so much the better, but our working lives don't always allow for this.

Remember that we are only talking about less than an hour. If there is a pool, a gym or a dance class on your way home, why not include this as part of your wind-down time? If running is more your cup of tea, head for a jog around the block before teatime – you could even get your kids involved! My best friend runs to and from work every day and she loves it.

A friend of mine recently set up a running club at his office, to allow his staff to begin the morning with a burst of energy before they start their working day. Maybe you could be part of developing something like this at your own workplace?

Letting the sunshine in

Sunshine is a subject of much deliberation. It is in fact *daylight* that allows the body to synthesise vitamin D, which we need daily, and can help to relieve conditions such as aching joints, asthma and the skin condition psoriasis. Whilst sunshine does have benefits, it's fair to say that these are more psychological. The physical effect of sun can be very harmful and it is important to understand that and to protect and nurture your skin.

Tanned skin is very much part of modern fashion. In the 1930s Coco Chanel was one of the first travellers to head to the South of France for the summer. Thus the notions of tanned skin and being rich enough for holidays became intertwined and the love for tanning began. (Prior to this pale skin was a sign of wealth; tanned skin had been associated with the workers outdoors.)

Staying safe in the sun ...

Whilst chatting to my Australian niece one morning sunbathing by the pool, she talked about how she didn't wear sunscreen on her face because she wanted to get a gorgeous tan. As I told her then, sunscreen does not prevent you from having a tan, but it will help to ensure that the sun does not play a part in accelerating your skin's ageing process.

Not protecting your skin from the sun may result in moles and age spots (brown pigmentation marks that appear on your skin over the years). Severe sunburn can result in brown moles immediately and you must have these checked to ensure that they do not contain or develop cancerous cells. If you live in a hot country it is extra-important to have

moles and marks checked regularly. It is also very important to protect any raised moles from the sun – cover them up with a generous amount of sun cream.

Our skin begins to mature from the young age of twenty-five, but don't wait until then to start protecting your skin – once fine lines begin they are hard to reverse. Using sunscreen every day will enable you to build up a gorgeous gradual tan whilst keeping your skin beautifully moisturised and youthful. It is extra-important to use it every day if you live in a country where the sun is always shining, putting it all over your body, but particularly on your face, beneath your foundation.

Many foundations now contain SPF (Sun Protection Factor) but remember you wear it all day and SPF does need to be topped up. Pat it onto your cheeks, forehead, nose, chin and neck with your fingertips to top up your skin throughout the day.

If you don't like the feel of sunscreen on your skin opt for a lightweight oil-free version – they aren't all thick and gloopy, there are some beautiful sunscreens out there. One of my favourites is made by Lancôme.

Don't forget your eyelids!

Your eyelids have such thin skin that they can burn quickly. Although we should avoid using moisturiser around our eye area, we can use sunscreen – it absorbs quickly and won't interfere with makeup as long as you use an eye primer before applying your eyeshadow, or a crease-free cream shadow. Alternatively, you can mix it in with your regular foundation and sweep it over your eyelids.

Don't neglect your hands

We apply sunscreen to our bodies and face using our fingertips or the palms of our hands, but the backs of our hands are often neglected. Our hands are exposed to UVA and UVB rays for much of the time, as well as to the ever-changing weather conditions, so it's important to keep them well moisturised and protected on a daily basis. After all, they are super important to us!

Drinking fluids

Drink at least six to eight glasses of fluid per day. Water is most effective and is a major part of staying healthy, and especially mentally alert. It helps concentration, which makes us work more effectively. I'm positive, also, that it really gives me a huge emotional lift.

Technology today means loads of air conditioning. Have you ever worn contact lenses in an air-conditioned office and found your eyes feeling dry? Imagine how much this is dehydrating your skin and your body! I don't know about you, but when I used to work in an office, I often found that with the cold air con I couldn't get thirsty enough to drink one of those little plastic cups of water – maybe it seemed like too much water in one go. Try taking a bottle of water to work instead. You'll find yourself drinking in sips and before you know it, you'll be filling it up again.

Relaxation

Relaxation is essential for a healthy, balanced mind. Stress does absolutely nothing for us, nor does worry. My husband once said to me, 'Relax with the world, and the world will relax with you.' In today's society we worry so much about so many things, and a lot of what we worry about is out of our control or completely imaginary! Believe it or not, we can *choose* to relax.

Maybe you have a high-powered job, you're a busy mum or you simply barely find time to relax and switch off from a busy lifestyle … Sometimes it's hard to draw a line between work and play.

Try sectioning your day into blocks. I find it really helps to think about my day this way: 'before 9am' = being mum time; '9am onwards' = working mum; '3pm/5pm onwards' = close the laptop, this is being mum time again; 'evening' = no work talk, this is relax time.

Try it and see if it works for you. Everyone is different, but at times life can feel so busy it's hard to organise it into a twelve-hour day. You'll probably find yourself shifting your work pattern and working efficiently enough to fit into these sections of time.

Having fun

Having fun, smiling and laughing are all really good for us and can actually affect the way that our skin looks. One phrase to remember is 'Feel good, look great!'

Having fun and staying relaxed have a huge impact on the way that we present ourselves. I'll never forget one period of time within my life when I suffered immense stress – not only did I lose weight, but my eyes looked tired, my skin pale and lifeless, my smile was less convincing and my eyes lost their sparkle. It sounds dramatic but it really is the truth. Our appearance is a huge part of feeling confident within, and I'm not talking about superficial things like white teeth and perfect hair. I mean the way that we hold ourselves when we walk, the way that we speak, the way that we interact with others, even the way that we stand still – do you play with your hands, shuffle your feet or generally become fidgety, or can you just 'be' still?

Whilst participating in an event one year in London I was thinking about this very section of my book, and I happened to be watching two air hostesses handing out leaflets. They stood strong, still and smart and oozed confidence. One air hostess had been up for thirty-six hours straight, but was so smiley that you would never have believed that she was tired: she looked beautiful.

Try slouching in your chair with a straight face … now sit up tall and grin – can you feel the difference? If you can, try implementing this within each area of your life. Nine times out of ten what we eventually realise after stressed periods within our lives is that actually by staying positive, things may not be that bad.

So how do I know this really works? From my own experience – it works for me, and I am confident that it will for you too. Stress, hunger, and tiredness often make you crave the unhealthy stuff like refined sugars and processed carbohydrates. These are quick fixes. What follows are sugar spikes that in turn send your mood up and then crashing down. The days when I don't exercise and eat unhealthily are low days for me. When I fill my days with activity (stimulation for the brain and social interaction), as well as eating well, cutting out refined sugars, replacing squash, fizzy drinks and fruit juices with water, sleeping well and exercising, I rapidly begin to feel on top of the world and full of energy. All of these things are involved in releasing serotonin, the happy hormone within the brain.

CHAPTER 3

Simple Steps to Beautiful Makeup

'Learn to feel beautiful without makeup on, and then begin to add touches of colour to your skin.'

Some people's skin will almost absorb makeup and such people may want to apply more, whilst others will only need a touch. See how just a little makeup makes you look even more beautiful, and then take this with you throughout each year of your life. A touch more here, a touch less there. As you age, add warmth to the colours that you choose, like using a warm peach blush instead of a cool pink, which will maintain a youthful glow as skin naturally becomes more sallow.

Makeup is like an illusion. There is so much that you can transform, exaggerate, highlight and conceal. Rather than applying products like you're just 'putting them on', try imagining your face as an art form and really sculpt the products to your features.

Once you are confident your makeup can take you as little as five minutes!

Always try to apply your makeup in some form of natural light as fake lighting makes everything appear softer and more yellow – meaning in daylight it could look like drag makeup. If you haven't got natural light available, step into a non-yellow light and check it. If you test foundations in a store, step outside to check the true colour match.

Applying makeup should be therapeutic, not a chore – have fun with it and really enjoy it. I don't know about you, but when I wake up in the morning I often feel sleepy, and then as soon as I put my makeup on, my body and mind goes 'ding' and I'm wide awake and feeling great. The same thing happens if I refresh my makeup throughout the day: it gives an instant uplift. My advice is to keep some mineral powder in your handbag, and if you ever feel like you might fall asleep at your desk, revitalise yourself with a sweep of magic powder!

Blending your makeup

You'll hear the word 'blending' a lot within the world of makeup, because it's probably one of the single most important aspects of a professional makeup application – it most

certainly makes the difference between great makeup and OK makeup. Even 'undone' makeup looks are applied with thought. Working quickly is a good way of achieving an undone eye-makeup because your lines may be less perfect than if you were to apply it slowly. With every look there is always blending to tie it together, whether it is soft shadow, smudgy lines, or definite lines and soft skin.

So often I see women wearing pink stripes of blusher, tide lines of foundation and patchy bronzer, not because they can't grasp professional technique, but because they don't fully understand how each product can be worn to produce its maximum effect.

Foundation should look invisible, and blusher should blend so seamlessly that it looks like naturally glowing skin. The only time that makeup should ever look hard is if it is meant to – like bold, strongly shaped eyeliner.

Creating a long-lasting base

- Use long-wear formulas that will stay put – the product description should give you an indication of durability. I am a lover of gel foundation for its lightweight, buildable, long-lasting finish. It gives radiance without the shine and is easily modified to create different textures using highlighters and mattifying products. Look for long-wear foundations with sheer, buildable coverage – thick formulas will sit on the surface of the skin and look cakey, whilst thin formulas allow you to build thin, longer-lasting layers.

- Avoid mixing oily products with water-based ones. When you tip oil into water, it sits and slides over the surface, and it can be the same with makeup – if you want your makeup to last, it's really important to use products that work together.

- Cleanse your skin with a product that's non-oily, as oily cleanser tends to sit on the surface of your skin and creates a barrier between your face and the makeup.

If you are a makeup artist and you need to cleanse skin quickly between models, keep water-based cleanser that can be used on eyes and lips as well as your skin handy, so that you can remove makeup quickly and comfortably. Oil-free wipes are a great quick fix, but I do find that if used too frequently on a model between looks it can make eyes feel a little sore, as you do have to use a bit more effort to remove makeup than with a true cleanser.

- If you find that your foundation slips throughout the day, use a serum foundation primer (not an oily cream one) instead of your usual moisturiser. If you have dry skin that doesn't tend to slip, you could opt for a hydrating cream primer. (Primers already have plenty of moisture in them, and that plus the natural oils in your skin that develop throughout the day, and the moisturiser within foundation, will be enough to keep your skin well hydrated.) It is actually possible to purchase foundations that already contain primer. Alternatively, you can mix a little primer into your foundation before applying it if you prefer not to apply primer as a separate layer.

  If you feel like you need something extra, ensure that you apply your moisturiser well before your foundation, allowing it time to sink into your skin.

- Using moisturiser at night is the most powerful time because the skin is at its most active, so during the daytime using a primer alone should be enough.

- Set your makeup with a lightweight powder. For extra staying power, spritz a fixing spray over your face prior to your foundation. You can also finish with it too.

- Apply all makeup layers in thin stages to avoid plastering it on too thickly, as layers that are too thick will slip, slide and melt away.

- Using a lip liner in conjunction with lipstick or lip-gloss will give it longer wearability.

Prep and prime

Apply a conditioning balm to the lips and allow it to work its magic whilst you apply the rest of your makeup. Remove any excess oil from the skin using a cotton wool pad and an oil-free cleanser. If you have used warm water to cleanse, follow with cold water to close the pores and plump up the skin. Choose a moisturiser that's right for

your skin and massage it into your face and neck using circular motions and avoiding the delicate eye area, which will be prepped instead with eye cream. The correct moisturiser will leave your skin looking radiant and youthful but not greasy or shiny. Ensure you choose one that benefits your own skin type. Allow this to sink in before priming, so that you avoid creating thick slippery layers that will slide over one another. Primer feels like silk on the skin and creates an ultra-smooth canvas on which to apply the rest of your makeup. It will help to minimise fine lines and enlarged pores.

Achieving a flawless complexion

Naturally radiant skin is always most glamorous. Women strive for beautifully blemish-free skin, which means not seeing that makeup has been used to create this. Bye bye, orange cake makeup!

Radiant, well-moisturised skin is key to an appearance of youthfulness.

Foundation does not fill in wrinkles and less is more! Uneven skin tone is more ageing than lines and wrinkles so this is what we want to focus on; even, bright skin really adds a vibrancy and youthfulness to your appearance.

Different makeup artists will tell you different things about what they feel is the most important area to concentrate on when applying makeup. The truth be told it's all of it, but for me, number one has to be complexion. If I'm in a rush, I'll pop on a tinted moisturiser, massage a gel bronzer or blusher into my cheeks and run out of the door feeling healthy –

lashes and lips bare but nevertheless feeling alive. Complexion is the one thing that really brings a face to life.

Achieving a flawless complexion is so easy to master once you know the tricks, and with a beautiful base you can choose to go nude on your eyes and lips or play with colour to make them pop. If you suffer from what you feel is problematic skin, never fear. Nine times out of ten when women say to me 'my skin is awful, it makes me feel so down' they actually only have certain areas of problematic skin, and the rest of the face is crystal clear. By keeping the coverage sheer over the clear areas of skin, and concentrating fuller coverage on problematic areas only, you will create the illusion of perfect skin.

One of my all-time favourite looks is the invisible makeup trick. Invisible foundation, cream bronzer, cream blush, a sweep of brighter blusher for a radiant glow, a sweep of mascara and a nude, ever so slight pink lip. Not everyone feels like they have time to spend beautifying in the mornings, and this look is perfect for a person at full speed.

If you want to brighten it up, use your finger to swipe a colour shadow across your lids, choosing a shade that really emphasises your own natural eye colour. (See page 55–6.)

Coverage
My secret to flawless skin that looks so real it could be
I recommend using sheer coverage and building it up in areas that need more. Always remember, foundation evens skin tone whilst concealer conceals. If you're using both, you shouldn't need a heavy foundation at all. Listed below are the various foundation types. Test the consistency on the back of your hand – it should sink into your skin and become invisible. If it sits on the surface like chalk or is hard to blend away, you can guess how it will sit on your face.

Full coverage
Never opt for full coverage in the hope of concealing blemishes; it will end up looking like a mask, with cakey patches all over the skin.

Sheer coverage
Sheer coverage is a lightweight formula, and is fantastic for mature and younger skins alike. It gives you the opportunity to build full coverage in the areas that need it, yet leave the great areas of your skin transparent for that gorgeous 'my skin is naturally this perfect' look.

Medium coverage
This lies between sheer and full coverage.

Selecting the right foundation formula

I find the best foundation for ageing skin to be a sheer coverage formula with a velvety finish and a soft gentle glow. Full coverage tends to have a thick consistency, which I find only emphasises wrinkles. Overly dewy products also highlight them, so an in-between formula like liquid to powder with sheen to its finish is perfect.

Crème

Rich and creamy, it gives a full and long-lasting coverage. It is very hydrating, so brilliant for extremely dry, or mature skin. Not an ideal formula for oily skin as it tends to become greasy very quickly and sits on the surface of the skin.

Mousse

A lightweight, hydrating formula. Mousse gives a sheer, buildable coverage. It suits almost all skin categories, other than very oily skin, as the textures do not combine well.

Liquid to powder

Medium coverage and a lovely velvety finish, it gives a beautiful pearl sheen.

Stick

Creamy in texture and very full coverage, it can be used as a concealer to cover blemishes and therefore is more appropriately used over small areas that need a little more coverage.

Powder

Feels very light on the skin, powder is buffed onto the skin to leave a soft, velvety finish.

Mineral powder foundation is very natural, and is kind on skin prone to breakouts, or oily skin, as the excess sebum is absorbed by the powder.

Gel

Gel foundation is a cross between liquid and cream in consistency. It is generally oil-free and very hydrating. It gives a sheer, buildable coverage.

Tinted moisturiser

Brilliant for dry or ageing skin, those who want an ultra sheer, summer glow, and teenagers who are just getting to grips with foundation (to avoid the plastered mask look). Tinted moisturiser has the sheerest coverage of all the foundation formulas. It gives skin more of a glow than coverage and really gives it a radiant lift. It is very hydrating and gives a youthful appearance, especially when used around the eyes, nose and mouth.

When you are choosing a tinted moisturiser, don't confuse illuminating with light reflective 'particles'. Illuminating will highlight wrinkles, whilst light-reflective particles will bounce light away from them.

Alphabetical creams

What are the differences between these letter-loving foundations-cum-tinted moisturisers?

BB cream stands for 'blemish balm', 'blemish base' or 'beauty balm'. It is an all-in-one product to replace serum, moisturiser, primer, foundation and sun block. The texture, consistency and coverage is similar to that of a tinted moisturiser and has buildable coverage. It also contains SPF.

CC cream stands for 'colour correcting', 'colour control' or 'complexion corrector'. This product offers the skincare benefits of a BB cream plus the ability to correct uneven skin tones such as redness, sallow skin or a lacklustre complexion.

DD cream stands for 'Dynamic Do It All' cream. This product is designed to prep, perfect and protect. The results are an immediate boost, and they also continue over time with a special focus on anti-ageing with claims to diminish fine lines and wrinkles.

Illuminating

This is foundation that has had illuminator added to it for a brightening effect on dull, tired skin. Illuminator also works well used as a sheeny highlighter. You can make your own illuminated foundation by taking your regular foundation and mixing illuminator into it on the back of your hand. But be warned that just as metallic shiny shadows emphasise wrinkles, I find that products with too much of a metallic finish do the same with mature skin, and can also emphasise large pores.

Choosing colours

Your foundation should be exactly the same colour as your natural skin tone. Often our faces are actually lighter than the rest of our bodies for several reasons. We are most likely to apply SPF to our faces. Also, we cleanse our skin very often. Bear in mind that pigment within skin varies from person to person; some people carry more pigment in certain areas, which is why pigmentation marks occur. With dark skin it is why the palms of the hands and the soles of the feet are lighter.

It can be hard to colour match against either face or neck so I always colour match against the chest, and check it against every visible part of skin to ensure that the colour looks perfect from head to toe.

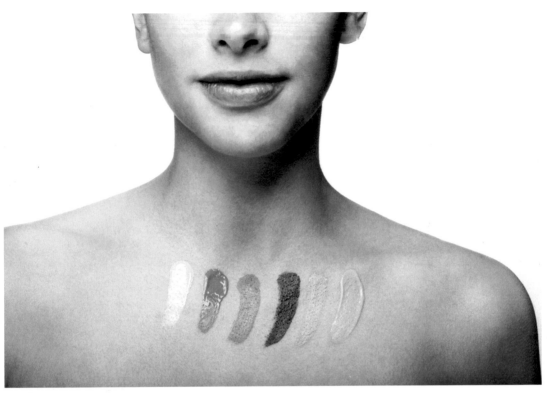

On occasion your chest may also be darker than the rest of your body, as natural tans are often deeper in some areas depending on how your skin tans and what you have been wearing. You can opt to tan the rest of your body with either a regular tanning product or an everyday gradual tan product, which will create a more uniform colour from head to toe.

If the rest of your body is darker than your face and neck, when you apply your correct shade to your face, it may look slightly darker than your neck does. In order to blend your neck into the rest of your body, buff bronzer from beneath your chin down the centre of your neck and also down either side from ear to collar bone.

Always buy a slightly yellow-based foundation (not orange and not banana yellow), avoiding at all costs a foundation with a pink tinge to it. Almost all people have yellow undertones within their skin, which means that if you use pink on top of it, it will stand out like a sore thumb and won't flatter your complexion. Using a yellow-based foundation reduces any redness or blemishes in the skin, keeps it warm, brightens tired eyes and emphasises everything beautiful about your skin. Hold the bottle up to your complexion: if it looks vibrant, it has the right tone; if it looks dull, it is likely to look chalky.

Sometimes the oils in our skin can change the colour of the foundation making it appear darker, so it's important to check this before investing. Most makeup counters will give you a tester to take away before you make the purchase of a huge bottle. It is a good idea to wear a new foundation for a couple of days and see how you get on with it.

Is your skin warm or cool?

Don't get too hung up on the cool or warm thing when it comes to foundation! The majority of skin tones have yellow undertones, and yellow-based foundations always look the most like real skin. I've heard it said that people with pink in their skin should use pink foundation, but I think this is a myth. Yellow-based foundation will counteract the redness in the skin, bringing it back to neutral.

There is an exception with dark skin tones that need blue-, red- or golden-based shades. Dark, cool skin tones (those with a slight blue or ashy tone) should opt for blue-based shades. Dark, warm skin tones (those with a golden or red tone) look best in golden-based or red-based shades.

I find the best way to determine your skin tone is to choose two bright colours, one blue-based, and one orange- or red-based. Hold them up to your skin, and whichever looks more flattering is most likely to tell you your skin tone.

Applying your foundation

Ensure that your skin is cleansed and that a foundation primer or moisturiser has been used before beginning to apply your foundation. Allow the skin to dry/absorb the product before beginning so that your foundation does not cling to the skin in patches.

Apply foundation from the centre of your face (your T-zone) and blend outwards until it becomes invisible. The centre of our face is the part that catches the eye and is generally the area where colour needs to be evened up. Very rarely do our faces need makeup at the very edge and this is better avoided, as it is what can create that mask-like effect.

Using a fluffy multi-use brush will create an airbrushed look, as it will stipple and blend the makeup whilst you twirl it over your skin, without the makeup settling into lines or pores.

Mattify the areas that you don't want to sheen – so your forehead, nose and chin. Don't try to cover blemished areas with layers of foundation as it just becomes cakey. Translucent, flawless skin is key to a beautiful complexion. Studying the texture of your skin is super important. Foundation should make a face appear sculpted, so avoid just 'putting' it onto the skin as it can end up looking flat. Instead, really look at the areas that need evening, and then use concealer to disguise areas that you would like to have more coverage. A mask of foundation can look terrible and false because certain areas of your skin will not need as much product as others. The older skin gets, the more evening out it needs, but the more lightweight the product needs to be. Whilst heavy products may give coverage, they also emphasise lines, making them look deeper than they actually are. Older skin is thinner, and thick foundation can cake and sit in lines.

If you find that you have large lighter and darker areas of skin throughout your face, again commonly seen in darker complexions, consider using more than one shade of foundation to even it out – for example, lighter over the darker areas and darker over the lighter so that you bring balance to the overall tone. You will need to colour correct the pigmentation marks first (see Foundation for black skin tones, below).

PRO TIP
Mix your foundation
For an accurate all-year-round complexion, mix your own shade. Buy the darkest and the lightest shades of your favourite foundation and mix the two colours together on the back of your hand to find and create your perfect match. Test the colour on your chest as you go – when it becomes invisible you have the correct shade. If you decide to wear fake tan one evening, you can mix up your new shade instantly.

Foundation for black skin tones
I recently did a makeup lesson with a lovely girl with beautiful black skin (note that she is not the model featured here). The biggest challenge she faces with her skin is large dark areas of pigmentation, which she hasn't always had and which had been distressing her somewhat. The problem she found was that if she applied her regular

foundation over the dark areas it would become ashy and grey-looking after a short time. I was able to teach her that it is a common misconception that you can disguise dark areas with a lighter foundation – the trick is to combat the colour first, to neutralise the dark so that you can bring the whole complexion back into one uniform skin tone.

The trick here is to use a vibrant orange corrector. Using a concealer brush or a foundation brush, buff it into the areas of dark only (not over your normal skin tone). Once the dark areas are neutralised and you are happy with the level of coverage, buff your regular foundation over these areas and the rest of your face. You will see that everything now looks one colour. Set this with powder and you are good to go! Don't forget to prime your skin first with a foundation primer so that this all remains in place. If you still need a little extra coverage, you can apply additional corrector on top of your foundation in areas that need it, ensuring that they are tied in perfectly to the rest of your skin tone.

Foundation for Asian skin tones

Asian skin tones tend to be quite yellow-based, although some have hints of red within them. I want to emphasise just how beautiful the Asian skin tone is, but getting foundation colour correct is absolutely fundamental to letting its beauty shine. If you put a shade that is too light onto it, it will look ashy and lifeless. Opt for yellow-based foundations as pink-based ones will simply not look natural. Also, avoid trying to whiten your skin as this can create a ghost-like effect. Embrace your skin tone!

Concealing, correcting and perfecting

Eliminating blemishes, spots and acne …

So, foundation evens out our skin tone and concealer evens out any blemishes – super crucial in creating airbrushed-looking skin. If you get really good at covering blemishes, it's even possible to create a perfect look without needing foundation – great for the days when you feel like letting your skin breathe.

Grasping this technique correctly is especially important if you suffer from acne, because using too much product can lead to caking, which actually makes your acne appear more obvious. It's also essential to colour match to your exact skin tone correctly – if you use a concealer that is too light, again it will actually make the blemishes, spots or acne more prominent.

Use your camouflage cream to perfect blemishes, patting the product directly onto the problem area using your fingers, blending it away at the edges and then stippling over with a thin brush to make blemishes completely disappear. Try not to cover freckles and beauty spots, as these are really beautiful characteristics and are what makes you unique.

Use a sheer to medium coverage foundation, and always avoid using a thick foundation if you suffer from lots of spots because 1. You want your skin to breathe, and 2. You actually want the areas of great skin to shine through, to compensate for the spots. Too much product over imperfections may look caked.

Dark or tired under eyes

Every woman suffers from this at some point, for varying reasons. Perhaps you are a mum suffering sleepless nights, maybe you have a busy work life, or maybe you like to party hard. Whatever the reason behind your tired eyes, I can teach you the art of disguising them perfectly …

Avoid wearing too much makeup under your eyes. The skin here is thin and doesn't absorb a great deal, and so product can look really obvious, especially if it is too thick.

Pop concealer onto the back of your hand first to allow it to heat up, before applying it to your under eyes, so that it literally blends into the skin. Never rub, only pat – rubbing will remove the product. Alternatively, when you apply product to your under eyes leave it to sit for a minute before blending it in.

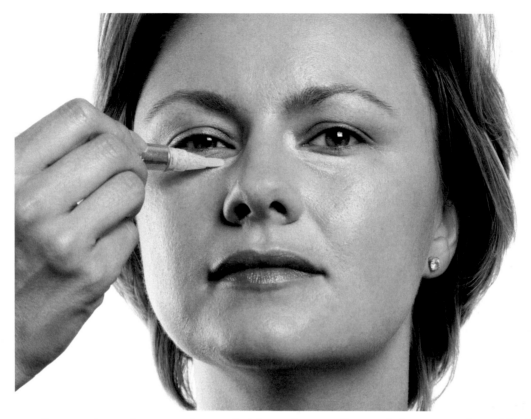

Correct the under-eye colour or brighten the area first, and then conceal to add a little more coverage and to bring your under eyes back to your normal skin tone.

Brighten your under eyes using an under-eye pen with a slight light-reflective pigment, or a yellow- or peach-based corrector to counteract any darkness. If your eyes are particularly dark, and you have fair skin, use a yellow-based corrector, followed by your natural skin tone concealer, focusing only on the dark areas.

If you have olive skin, use a peach corrector followed by your natural tone of concealer and if you have dark skin, use orange followed by your natural skin tone concealer. You can go one shade lighter than your natural skin tone for extra brightness, however I often think it appears disconnected from the rest of the face once your blusher is on, so I prefer to use a shade of concealer that matches the rest of the face. Be cautious about the colour that you are applying here: the under-eye skin is lighter and more blue in tone due to its transparency – colours can show up more orange, too yellow, or too white and ashy – so be sure to colour match here correctly.

If you find the area is too light, use a light pat of your usual foundation over the top of it to avoid panda white eyes.

Some people have particularly red skin around their eyes. If this is you, be sure to take your under-eye concealer right up to the lash line, and use mascara or eyeliner along the lower lash line to open up the eye. Using concealer right up to the lash line without added definition can make eyes appear smaller.

If you have any ageing under your eyes or they are particularly sensitive, try using your normal foundation alone with a slightly lighter shade mixed into it for a brightening effect. Pat it beneath your eyes very softly, or use a very lightweight under-eye pen.

Dab a pea-sized amount of tinted moisturiser around your eyes to plump the skin, give a youthful appearance and to help minimise fine lines and wrinkles. (This should be non-illuminated. Illuminating fine lines and wrinkles will do exactly as it suggests.)

If you have fine lines, wrinkles or dry skin don't overload this area, use just a very small dot on the tip of your finger and pat it into the inner corner of your under eyes.

Alternatively, you can follow the socket line of your under eyes – the line of shadow that runs in a semi-circle – using just a line of concealer, blending it into that area alone. This means that you will be brightening the area, but won't be overloading the skin. The result will look far more youthful because the concealer won't have collected in any fine lines. This is a great trick even for younger people who find that their skin is such below the eyes that the makeup here creases during the day.

Pop a small dot of highlighter onto the inner corner of your eyes (the tear ducts). This will give them an instant lift. As eyes age the inner corners don't really tend to wrinkle, so there's no need to worry about exaggerating creases. This is a lifelong tip for wide-awake, sparkling eyes.

Set your under-eye makeup with a light dusting of translucent powder to prevent it from creasing – ensure that this is very minimal to avoid the powder caking or emphasising lines. Use a fluffy eyeshadow blending brush, tap off the excess powder and sweep the brush gently beneath the eyes – you will notice it creating smooth, crease-free skin.

Puffy eyes

One question asked by so many women is why have I got puffy eyes and how can I cover them?

The first thing to understand is that you cannot cover puffy eyes. You can create an illusion of them not being there, but because the skin is raised, even makeup won't make them totally disappear. Avoid using a light-reflective product, as this will emphasise them. Where possible, leave them makeup-free and simply blend the rest of your foundation around your eyes to ensure that your under eyes don't look obviously makeup-free in comparison to the rest of your face. A little trick for reducing their appearance is to take a fine concealer brush and run concealer just along the underside of the puffy area where you can see a darker line. Sit in front of a mirror, tilt your head towards the floor and but look up into the mirror – you will be able to see where this line of shadow falls. You can also see it beneath ceiling spotlights that shine down on us from above, which is why some mirrors appear to be more flattering to us than others – it's not the mirror's fault, it's actually the lighting, so rest assured you look beautiful.

Continuously puffy eyes (rather than temporary ones after a heavy night) are actually caused by a layer of fat underneath the skin. The reasons behind permanently puffy eyes vary – it can be genetic, or caused by your lifestyle, or just by ageing.

Your eyes naturally sit in pads of fat to protect them and as you age, the membrane between your eyes and the pad deteriorates and fat cells escape.

Other factors include high cholesterol, smoking, drinking, not sleeping properly and drug abuse. Allergies and fluid retention can also cause puffy eyes. Puffy eyes are hard to get rid of, but for those with a very severe case there is plastic surgery – a drastic step which needs to be considered very carefully.

If your puffy eyes are genetic they may become more apparent as you age because as this happens the skin on the face starts to droop, revealing aspects that may not have been previously visible.

There are things that you can do to help prevent this condition developing or to encourage it to lessen, if it is already apparent:

– Keep well hydrated
– Cut down on salt
– Facial massage – drainage of the lymph glands
– Good diet
– Limited caffeine
– Exercise

Start using eye creams from a young age – yes, even twenty! This ensures that your under eyes will stay strong throughout the years to help prevent them from sagging and bagging so much in the future.

If you don't have puffy eyes consistently but find that you get them every now and then through tiredness, simply pop an ice cube into a napkin and hold it against your eyes to reduce the puffiness.

Age spots (hyper-pigmentation)

I think you can embrace age spots and treat them as you would a beauty spot, just be sure to use sunscreen on them daily to keep them well protected. However, if you would like to cover them and you have fair skin, use a yellow corrector. If you have dark skin, use an orange corrector.

Dot the corrector over the age spot ensuring that you only cover the area that is dark. Use your finger to pat around the edges of where you have corrected.

Now stipple foundation over the area – do not wipe, because you will wipe away the work you have just done. Set the product using a dusting of translucent powder.

Use this same technique if you suffer from dark pigmentation marks that cover large areas of skin – this often occurs in Asian skin types, and in some cases throughout pregnancy.

Sometimes people have a condition which results in light patches rather than dark. This is actually a loss of pigmentation within the skin.

To bring these back to your natural skin colour you will need to use a concealer that is the colour of your natural skin colour, and apply it within the area that is lighter. Set this with translucent powder once done. Repeat as necessary for complete coverage.

Rosacea

Rosacea is reddened skin that commonly covers the high points of the face – cheeks, nose, forehead and chin – but with today's yellow-based foundations it is easily disguised. Some women find that their skin will flare up with certain products, others suffer with the condition constantly and many women develop it as they age.

Years ago thick green concealers were used to hide rosacea. Scrap these; they make your skin look dull and chalky. Instead opt for either a gel moisturiser like Dermalogica Redness Relief, which contains a hint of green, prior to your foundation, and follow with your usual foundation. Or, for more severe cases or if you wish for more coverage, pat a yellow concealer over areas of reddened skin. Follow by stippling foundation over the same areas to bring it back to your real skin tone. Set with translucent powder.

Thread veins

Broken veins and capillaries are very common as the skin ages, and can also occur in young skin.

First, use a small brush to trace over the vein with concealer, and then set with translucent powder.

Creating a bronzed look

Blushing and bronzing

> **HELPFUL HINT**
> Keep blush and bronzer high on the face for a youthful glow.

Bronzer

Bronzing products are available in the form of:

– Powder

– Cream

– Gel

– Mousse

– Tint

Everyone, from the palest to the darkest of skin tones, can benefit from bronzer. It is such a fabulous product not only for creating the appearance of a tan, but simply for adding a healthy glow to the skin.

Matt bronzers always look the most natural and if you are prone to blemishes or spots it is best to avoid shimmery products which can often draw attention to problem areas. Matte bronzer will not only help to even out your skin tone, but may also appear to make breakouts recede – choose a mineral bronzer that will give your breakouts some TLC.

When choosing a bronzer it is very important to select one with your correct skin tone. You need to assess the colour of your complexion and of the skin on the rest of your body before deciding what shade of bronze to use on your face.

If you have pale white, peachy white or golden skin, honey colours are lovely. Avoid brown bronze where possible because it can look muddy on a pale complexion.

Olive skin looks great with a caramel tan and this will counteract any ashy sallow skin tones. Orange- or golden-toned bronzers also look beautiful.

Deeper orange- or red-toned bronzers flatter deep golden bronze skin tones.

Applying bronzer lightly over your cheekbones and temples will create a soft, subtle glow.

Beautifully bronzed

The key to a gorgeous tan is for it to appear completely natural, and to gradually flow in tonal range throughout the highlights and shadows of your face and body. For this you need to understand exactly how our skin tans.

So often I see women who have bronzed to the point where it looks completely flat. This is because they tan every area of their body in one colour. When we go on holiday, there are always areas that tan more darkly than other areas. For example, the high points of our faces like cheeks, forehead, etc, whilst the areas that fall in shadow like our necks often take longer to tan, if they tan at all.

Notice when you have a real tan that the colour is not flat, it looks sculpted with the shape of your face and body. Have you ever noticed that you can sometimes tell when a woman is wearing fake tan because the underneath of her arms looks as dark as the tops of them? The sun doesn't catch the underneath of our arms as it does the top; therefore the colour should gradually fade from one side to the other.

Fake tan is super, and the way forward for today, with all the knowledge we have about the sun causing skin cancer. There's nothing wrong with people knowing you're

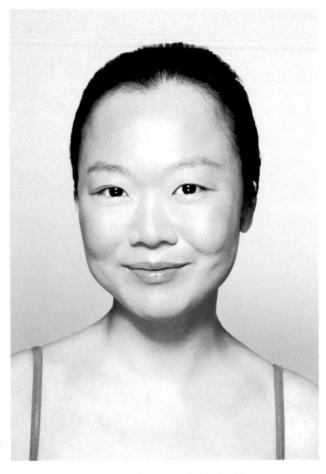

wearing it, but it looks even more gorgeous when it's so perfect that it looks like your own, golden skin tone.

When you create a tan on your face, *always* bronze your body too; every area of skin that can be seen should be a match to your face for it to look completely real.

You want people to look at you and think, 'Wow, she looks gorgeously tanned' and not 'Wow, she's wearing fake tan!'

Because faces are often lighter than necks and the rest of our bodies, it's important to colour match it into the rest of our bodies before beginning to bronze.

If your face is darker than the rest of your body, avoid trying to lighten it because this can look ashy and make a complexion 'washed out'. Instead, bronze your neck and décolletage area, which will extend the glow from face to chest.

In order to create the most amazing, natural tan, we should mimic the way the sun naturally tans us – first, the sun turns the skin slightly pink and then it becomes golden or bronze. Because of this, I apply blush before bronze.

How to do it:

- Mist your face with foundation that matches exactly the colour of your chest/body.

- Apply under-eye corrector to brighten your eyes, then pat a small layer of concealer over the top of this to blend it in with your natural skin tone.

- Buff a deep or vibrant pink or red cream blush onto the tops of your cheekbones and a tiny amount on the high points of your face where the sun would catch you (hairline, nose, chin, cheeks, shoulders).

- Press translucent powder into your skin all over using a cotton pad to make it velvety-smooth. It's super important when bronzing that it glides on and doesn't cling in patches.

- Sweep matte bronzer along the cheekbone, keeping the colour high.

- Sweep it up around your temples where the sun would naturally hit, down the bridge of your nose, along your jawline/chin and down onto your neck.

- Pop a sheer amount of translucent powder onto your powder brush and buff all over your skin to blend everything seamlessly. Ensure that you sweep beneath your eyes to avoid white panda marks. Using the brush with a left to right sweeping motion will taper the colour down the face in a gradual, natural way.

- Sweep shimmer highlight over your cheekbones to give them luminosity and three dimensions.

- Tidy your brows and apply mascara to your top lashes. Touch the lower lashes gently for colour definition. Finally, apply a tinted balm to your lips.

PRO TIP

For the ultimate party glow, add a shimmery bronze to your lower lash line, define your upper lash line with liner and smudge it out using the same shimmery bronze. Apply mascara and finish with a natural lip-gloss.

Applying blusher

Blusher products are available in the form of:
– Powder
– Cream
– Mousse
– Tint

I believe that good blusher makes a 'look' more classy. So many times I have seen women overdo it – gorgeous eye makeup, a gorgeous lip colour and then … two bright pink stripes of pink or brown. Colour is designed to be seen, but the reason why blushers are designed in shades of peach, plums, pinks, oranges and bronzes is because they are created to reflect and accentuate the colour of our natural skin tone. Blusher should be subtle, but truly glowing.

If I were trapped on a desert island and could choose just one product, it would be blusher. (Actually, it would be a two-in-one lipstick/cheek product that doubles up as a blusher for double the gorgeousness!) Blusher gives sallow or tired skin radiance.

Look at yourself in the mirror at home with no makeup on. Pop blusher on one side of your face and not the other. See how alive the side with blusher looks?

My favourite are cream blushers for their healthy, natural glow. They have that slightly dewy finish which has such a nourishing, youthful appearance. I like to apply blusher before bronzer, so that it gives a real 'from within the skin' glow. I also like to finish a look with an extra pop of vibrant blusher just on the top of the cheekbone to give the skin an extra boost of radiance.

There are some key tips for getting blusher right that I will share with you:

• For a tanned complexion, the most flattering blushers are apricots and peaches or warm, vibrant pinks. If you suffer from rosacea, the yellow undertones of peach or apricot will help to reduce the redness.

• Dark complexions look beautiful in deep or bright blusher shades – plums, pinks, burgundy oranges and bronzes. Avoid light or pastel shades, which may look chalky.

• Use a blusher with sheen for three dimensions. Matte blushes can look flat and ageing.

• If you have ageing skin, swap pinks for peaches (peaches lift sallow skin and help to accentuate a look of youth, whilst pinks may wash sallow skin out further) and keep all blusher and bronzing products high to lift the face and give an appearance of youthfulness. Remember the skin drops but our cheekbones stay in the same place as they have always been. For the most natural result, keep the shade as close to your natural blushing colour as possible.

The way you apply your blusher can change your appearance from soft to strong. For example, if you blend blusher onto the apples of your cheeks it will give you a flush of youth and health, whilst keeping colour towards your temples is a stronger look.

Keep in mind what eye makeup you are wearing when you apply your blusher. If dark and intense, keep the colour further to the perimeter of the face. The eyes should be the focal point.

If your eyes are more neutral or colourful in shade, sweep the blusher more onto the apples of your cheeks for a fresh, fun and pretty feel.

For brides, I recommend using blusher on the apples of your cheeks for a radiant, healthy, pretty glow.

I love colour to shine through from within, so I tend to choose the area where I would most like to see colour, whether closer to the temples and along the cheekbone or on the apple of the cheek, and begin in that place and blend it away to nothing towards the less focal area. So for example, when I create pretty apple cheeks, I focus on the apple of the cheek and blend away to nothing towards the temples.

Contrary to popular belief, it is not very effective to smile when you apply your blush because as you smile, your muscles lift and as soon as you stop smiling, the muscles drop again, leaving you with blusher halfway down your face! Smiling when applying blush can also be instantly ageing – as you smile, product can miss the areas in which your skin creases, and when you relax, you are left with areas of skin that have not grabbed the product which can look like wrinkles, even if you don't really have them.

Lastly, try to avoid using bronzer alone on the cheeks, as it can look a little unnatural or muddy on its own. Naturally we all have a flush of colour within our cheeks which makes us look healthy. If you do want to use bronzer alone, choose two shades for a little more definition, one applied as a base colour and the second as a pop of colour on the apples of your cheeks or along the cheekbones. You can use a fine shimmer too for a little extra sculpting (contrary to belief, this looks beautiful on ageing skin – just keep it minimal and only to the apple of the cheek, then the light reflection creates a slight fullness and roundness there which mimics that of youth).

How to apply cream blush

Step one
Dot blush onto the mid to top part of your cheekbone nearest to the apple of your cheeks (the cushiony part).

Step two
Blend the blush out over the apples of your cheeks and up towards your temples.

Step three
Use the warmth of your fingers to really mesh the product with your skin.

I love using lipstick as a cream blush to really make the lip colour pop. I first discovered this after going swimming – I had nothing but foundation and a lipstick in my bag, so thought I'd give it a go! With such a huge colour spectrum of lipsticks available you can really have fun with this.

Applying powder blush

Lightly dust the face with face powder (translucent or pressed – used for reducing shine and setting foundation) and then apply powder blush using a blush brush with a pointed tip. With the tip of your bristles, use soft sweeping movements as if you are painting the cheekbone. Take a big powder brush and blend over this using a circular motion to ensure it looks flawless, like a 'from within the skin' glow.

53

Powder

Opt for either translucent or a yellow-based powder (the most natural undertone for almost all skin types other than deep skin tones which sometimes have red or blue undertones, in which case you'd opt for a deeper tinted face powder).

Knock excess powder off on the back of your hand before applying it, starting from the perimeter of your face and working your way in so that you don't apply too much product to the centre of your face, unless you are only focusing on the T-zone (centre of the face). If you have enlarged pores, especially on your nose, a good trick is to roll or press a powder puff over the area, creating an illusion of smaller pores.

Remember that no matter what the product, light-reflective properties will always illuminate the area that you are trying to disguise – it is far more effective to opt for products that give a more matte finish. When purchasing a powder, try to avoid any talc-based products – talc is one of the most ageing products that you can put on your skin, particularly because it can really dry the skin out.

Applying eyeshadow

One of the key elements to a beautiful makeup look is the eye makeup. I am a strong believer that everyone can wear any colour or style of eyeshadow that they like, if they chose the shade or undertone that suits them and follow their natural eye shape. As women age, eye makeup has the power to lift and enhance the eyes. Contours in the socket line should be soft and shadow-like, whilst colour and density looks best worn close to the lash line, where it enhances definition and makes the eyes look powerful.

Choosing the right colour

I hear so often women saying, 'I wish I could wear that colour but it doesn't suit me'. Within the colour palette we have our basic colours – blue, red, purple, green etc. By establishing what shade and undertone suits you, you can confidently wear any colour that you like.

There are two basic guidelines that you can follow when choosing colour:

Shade

Choose the shade that suits you: for example, pastel, vibrant, deep. Hold the colour next to your eyes. If it looks dull or chalky against your skin then it's not for you; if it looks rich against your skin, it is a winner. The right shade should look great whether it's worn alone or with other makeup.

Undertone

Every colour has an undertone – orange based (warm), blue based (cool) and finally, neutral, which has a mixture of both warm and cool undertones within it. This undertone suits everyone (mahogany is an example of a neutral colour). To establish which undertone suits you, hold the colour up to your eyes. If it makes your complexion glow or your eye colour pop, it's going to be a great colour for you.

Makeup artists often use a colour wheel as a quick way of determining which colour is likely to enhance a person's eye colour. This colour wheel is comprised of complementary colours. Complementary colours sit opposite one another on the colour wheel: they are pairs of colour which, when placed next to each other, create the strongest contrast and reinforce each other. The colour wheel, when divided in half, gives us our warm and cool colours.

Bronze, gold, orange, peach and yellow all look fantastic worn next to blue eyes. Blue-toned colours lighter or darker than your eye colour also look amazing.

Purple and red greatly enhance green or hazel eyes. Hazel eyes with yellow flecks can be emphasised with orange-based bronzes or yellow-based golds.

Brown is considered a neutral colour so brown eyes suit most colours, while purple, blue and green really enhance them.

Brown, grey and black are neutral colours that look good with all eye colours.

Eyeshadow textures and finishes

The two main categories for eyeshadow are **cream** (a velvety-smooth formula that goes on easily with a finger or brush) and **powder**; these come in a variety of finishes:

Matte. A silky, matte formula glides on smoothly and blends easily. As you age, these look best worn in the socket line, whilst pearl shadow looks great on the lower eyelid.

Pearl. Pearl shadow has a beautiful three-dimensional sheen to it without looking glittery or metallic. It flatters all ages and skin tones and types.

Shimmer. Sheer, lightly pearlised shadow. Often it has a very translucent finish, and looks beautiful worn alone, or over a more opaque eyeshadow.

Metallic. The high-shimmer, high-pigment formula metallic eyeshadows look best worn on the lower eyelid at any age. They are light-reflective and tend to illuminate lines and creases and therefore can make eyes appear more heavily lined than they actually are.

Sparkle. Shimmering pearls and fine glitter.

When you are choosing your eyeshadows, test the colour on your fingertip – it should look vibrant immediately. If you find that you have to scrub your finger back and forth to get any colour to adhere or to make it vibrant it is not worth the investment, as it means that it has low pigment content, and trying to blend and build up colour on your eyes would take forever and could get messy. You want to invest in shadows that are vibrant and soft like velvet from the start.

A trick to test the blending is to pop the shadow on the back of your hand using your finger, and then take a second shade and overlap it onto the other. If the edges blend easily into one another they should be fabulous to work with on your eyes. Similarly check that the texture isn't so soft that when you blend them together they blend away!

Stay-proof eyeshadow

Do you find that your eyeshadow creases during the day? That's because our eyelids are one of the oiliest parts of our face. Avoid applying moisturiser to your eyelids, the natural oil is plenty enough and the skin is so thin here that it won't be able to absorb it all, leaving it floating on the surface. Try wiping any excess oil away with a little cleanser on a cotton wool pad, and then use your fingertip to apply a small amount of eyeshadow primer, concealer or long wear shadow in your skin tone over the top of it. This will keep any eyeshadow that you apply on top of this in place and make it easy to blend. It also helps to even out the colour of your eyelids; the skin here is thin and more translucent than the rest of the face.

The only time you don't need to set your eyelids with powder is if you are going to be using a cream shadow.

HELPFUL HINT

To determine where your eyeshadow should end on your eyes, especially if you are creating a winged-out effect, place a brush against your nose and hold it diagonally up to the outer corner of your eye – the eyeshadow should end at this marker. Bear in mind that when you blend eyeshadow it spreads it out further, so stop just short of where you want it to end before you start to blend. Going any further beyond this line risks losing that lifted appearance.

To give eyes even more of a lifted appearance, move the brush in an up-and-outward motion when you are blending to keep the colour heading in the correct direction.

Always use the tip of your brush with a gentle touch, applying too much pressure will cause the bristles to splay out, ultimately altering the shape of your makeup. This is particularly important when you are blending through the crease (socket line) of your eyes.

The no-eyeshadow, eyeshadow application

This is a very basic technique for subtly enhancing your eye shape and is perfect for those of you who love the no makeup, makeup look, and for giving ageing or hooded eyes an instant lift. Pat a light skin-toned shadow over your eyelid and blend the shade into the socket line. Take an eyeshadow a couple of shades darker than your skin tone (a matte bronzer could also work well) and looking straight on into a mirror, gently blend it into your socket line (the crease) using the tip of the bristles of a fluffy eyeshadow brush (blending brush). Sweep the brush back and forth through the socket line in a sort of windscreen wiper motion to follow the natural curve of your eyes. It is particularly important to look straight forward into a mirror as you do this if you have hooded or ageing eyes because as the skin drops so does your eyeshadow – this way you can ensure that the eyeshadow is being applied in the correct place.

Curl your lashes – pump for ten seconds and then walk the curlers up halfway and do the same thing: this will give them a natural curve rather than bending them. Always curl your lashes before you put on your mascara for a separated finish. Run mascara from the root to the tips of your lashes, wiggling the wand as you go.

Smoky eyes

Smoky eyes are often the most difficult look to master. If it goes wrong we can end up looking like we've been punched in the eyes. However, when it is applied correctly the result is hot!

I was asked specifically to include this look in my second book, particularly for the mature woman wondering what technique she should be using. This technique of tapering eyeshadow creates a new depth and dimension to the shadows of the eyes, bringing the eyes

forward, opening them up and creating absolute definition. This isn't the only reason why the smoky eye has become one of the most featured looks of today: it is so diverse, and there are many ways that you can adapt a smoky eye to define your eyes perfectly.

Often we find an image and try to copy the shading exactly – scrap this, your eye shape needs specific personalised contouring in order to maximise its shape completely. For the most flattering shape, follow your socket line exactly. Winging eyeshadow outwards elongates the eyes, whilst creating a rounder shadow opens the eyes up. To create an elongated eye, blend the shadow out in the direction your lower lash line follows. If you stop just short of where you want the final shadow to finish, your blending will finish it in the correct place.

59

Everyday smoky eyes

Prime your eyelids with eye primer or concealer (gently pat this over the eyelid).

Apply a deep brown eyeliner along the upper and lower lash line.

Take a medium brown eyeshadow and apply it over the eyeliner. Blend it over your eyelid, into your socket line and following the shape of your eyes, pull it up and out slightly at the end of your eye. Open your eye and using a fluffy eyeshadow brush, sweep left and right in a windscreen wiper motion through the socket line to ensure that there are no harsh lines. The colour should fade gradually towards the brow bone.

Sweep a bone-coloured eyeshadow lightly beneath the brow bone to define the shape. (Try to avoid using shimmer here because it can look very old fashioned.)

Apply mascara from the roots of your lashes to the tips and finish the look by softly defining your brows.

HELPFUL HINT

You can use any shade eyeshadow to create this look, from brown, silver and black to any other colour in the rainbow!

For extra drama, use a kohl pencil to define the water line and to add further definition to the upper and lower lash line.

Experiment with new textures – cream and metallic has a beautiful finish. Keep metallic shadows close to the lash line.

Dark smoky eyes with a hint of colour entwined within them have a beautiful, sultry effect.

Apply black kohl eye-liner to your upper lash line; blend it all over the lower eyelid, stopping within your socket line. Pat a black shimmer shadow over the eyeliner and blend into the socket line. Blend a purple eyeshadow through the socket. Line over the top of the black and extend beyond it slightly so that the colour fades into the other. Sweep the same purple along the lower lash line.

Smoky eye makeup for hooded and monolid eyes

A monolid is when the socket line is not defined, your upper eyelid covers your lower eyelid. This can make it more difficult to apply eye makeup so that it can be seen. Hooded eyelids form in much the same way and the amount of lower eyelid that can be seen will vary from person to person.

Step 1

- Lift the hood of the eye and apply a cream shadow all over the under eyelid. Open your eyes and look straight into a mirror. Place your eyeshadow brush into your socket line (you can gently feel where this is with your fingertips) and sweep the brush left and right using a windscreen wiper motion to create a marker where your socket line should be.

Step 2

- Pat a light shimmery shadow onto the centre of your eyelid to highlight the eye.

Step 3

- Apply your darkest shade on the outer edge and the inner corner of your eyelid. What you darken and make matte recedes, which is perfect for hooded eyes, creating an illusion of a defined lower eyelid.

Step 4

- A great tip to achieve the perfect shape for Asian eyes – look up to the ceiling, sweep the darkest shadow from the upper outer corner of the lash line in a 'V' motion down and around to the bottom outer corner of your lower lash line. Sweep back and forth until the colour is dense enough.

Step 5

- Line the upper lash line with a push liner brush and gel liner; press the product into the lash line. Turn your head side on to the mirror and press the brush from the lower lash line outwards, following its direction to create a marker. Take a felt-tip liner or a fine-tip eyeliner brush, put the point against the end of that marker and pull in towards your upper lash line – this will create a lovely kitten flick.

Step 6

- Soften the eyeliner along the upper lash line by smudging your darkest eyeshadow along it.

Step 7

- Curl your lashes and apply two or three coats of mascara to your top and bottom lashes. Wiggle the wand at the root for extra definition. Don't wait for each coat to dry before applying the next as this can cause clumpy lashes. Instead, coat one eye three times, followed by the next.

Steps 8 and 9

- Apply a peach blusher to your cheeks and finish off with a vibrant lipstick in orange-based red or coral.

Applying pro liner

My favourite eyeliner application is achieved by pressing eyeliner into the root of your lashes. This gives an illusion of thicker lashes, and will ensure that your entire lash line is dense in colour, with no gaps when you open your eyes. You can apply this very finely for a subtle look, or apply more product or a darker shade for more emphasis. If you want a soft smoky effect, try pressing eyeshadow over the top of the liner. If you want to create a more dramatic eyeliner line, you can press the product along the lash line in stages as normal. Once you have a guide, you can draw a clean line along the root of the lashes, and for a thicker line up, onto the eyelid.

- Gel eyeliner won't drag your skin, has amazing pigment intensity, won't smudge once dry and is so easy to apply, with its thick consistency. I also like to use eyeshadow wet for dense application or dry for soft eyeliner shading. Any eyeshadow colour and texture can be transformed into eyeliner.

- Felt-tip eyeliners are amazing for creating solid lines or winged eyeliner flicks.

- Kohl pencil is lovely on the lower lash line or along the water line. If you find your eyeliner moves into the tear ducts of your eyes, waterproof eyeliner may be more effective.

There are lots of eyeliner colours available. Hold a colour up to your eyes and if it makes them pop, it will look beautiful and make a statement.

Eyeliner flicks – the secret revealed

I'm really excited to reveal this secret, because it's so simple!

For years I struggled with achieving the perfect flick on each eye with no wobbles, even as a makeup artist. I tried every technique under the sun and still found that it did not guarantee a symmetrical flick, until I came across the world's most simple trick.

1. Take a push liner brush. Turn your head side on to the mirror. Place the push liner brush on the outer edge of your eye, following the lower lash line to create a marker guideline.

2. Take a felt-tip liner (I love using these for their sturdy, fine tip) and leaning the pen slightly on its side, place the tip onto the end of the marker you have just made and pull towards your upper lash line.

3. Fill in the gaps.

4. Looking up, ensure the underside of the flick joins with your eye so that there are no gaps.

If you struggle with this technique because you find that your eyes crease, once you have

made the marker, look straight ahead into a mirror and trace the lines in with a kohl pencil. Once you are happy that it's sitting in the right place, you can trace over it with a gel or felt-tip eyeliner, which is designed not to smudge.

Applying your eyeliner whilst wearing glasses

This was a specific request from my lovely friend Paula's mummy, Lesley. There are lots of makeup tutorials on what makeup suits women with glasses of various frame sizes and colours, but not many that actually tackle the issue of applying it whilst you are wearing glasses. For those of you who don't wear contact lenses, but have the challenge of applying makeup day to day with a magnifying mirror to compensate, trying to fight your way around the glasses and avoid looking like a primary school painting for lack of vision, where there is a will, there is a way! I too wear glasses from time to time when I'm not wearing my contact lenses and so this is my tried and tested technique:

The upper lash line: Place a mirror (this can be regular as you are wearing your glasses – hurrah!) on a table or flat surface in front of you. Looking down into the mirror, place your eyeliner on your eyelid from beneath the glasses and apply as you normally would – basically, you will need to keep the eyeliner tilted at an angle, so this may take a few tries to master. If you find it difficult going from the underneath, move your glasses down towards the tip of your nose (go as far as you can while you can still see properly). Now fill in your upper lash line.

The lower lash line: Hold the mirror up high, look up into the mirror and line your lower lash line from beneath the glasses.

Applying eyeshadow and mascara works the same way: it's all about finding the technique that works for you.

Creating lovely lashes

Eyelashes are amazing! Natural or false, they create a finish for your eye makeup; they can even create an eye makeup look on their own, without the support of eyeshadow. It is very rare (unless you have hugely long and thick dark lashes) for mascara to create the kind of eyelashes that we see in all of the mascara adverts. This is because generally these adverts use false lashes and/or digital enhancement.

I find natural defined lashes look the most flattering teamed with really fresh eye makeup, or with very dark eye makeup. So much length and density can be created purely through the power of a good mascara and eyeliner.

When you are younger you can rock nude eyes with nude lashes. As you age, it's really important to focus on your lashes because they really open up your eyes, drawing attention to your best features. This is where false lashes are super.

How you use your mascara wand, believe it or not, is key to the final appearance of your eyes. The angle at which you point the wand will change the finished effect.

For example, as your eyes begin to age you want to make them appear as uplifted as possible, therefore the shape of your eye should be wide. To achieve this you need to hold your mascara wand horizontally against the lashes, wiggle it at the root and then bring it straight up through the lashes.

Maximise the length of your lashes by using a lash primer followed by two mascaras – lengthening first, followed by volumising. Avoid pumping your mascara wand in the tube as this pumps air into it, which can cause it to dry out. Instead twist and pull to open it, twist and push to close it.

New makeup colours and formulas are being launched all the time, it's really about trial and error and what works for you. Wherever possible ask the artist at a counter to trial some on you so that you walk away with a mascara that you feel helps you to achieve the look that you desire.

Create flirty lashes

Sweep your mascara out to the side. To elongate your eyes, trim a pair of strip lashes and apply the outer edges to the outer edges of your own lashes.

Define your lashes (*upper and lower*)

Perfect for young or mature eyes, however take note of your under eyes – if they are particularly dark or creased you will want to keep this area as fresh and clear as possible, which would mean dramatising the top lashes and leaving the lower lashes nude or coated with a clear mascara. Wiggle the mascara wand at the root of your lashes for a couple of seconds before you wiggle it up to the tips.

Natural lashes

Perfect for eyes at every age, a very soft, pretty look. Sweep mascara from root to tip. Lightly touch the bottom lashes to give them some colour.

If your eyes are mature pay extra attention to those top lashes to ensure that they are really lifted. The ultimate aim for any eye is to make it appear wide-awake and uplifted.

Stop your mascara smudging

A frequent complaint is that over the day mascara transfers or flakes onto your upper eyelids or beneath your eyes. This is particularly common the more we age and the more the eyes begin to crease, as it becomes increasingly tricky to apply eye makeup. There are a few tricks to try and prevent smudging from happening.

Apply your lower lash mascara first and allow it to dry. Next, apply your upper lash mascara and allow it to dry before you fully open your eyes. If you apply mascara to the top lashes first and look up to do your lower ones the first thing that can happen if you have long lashes is that it will smudge onto your upper eyelid – pretty annoying if you've already blended beautiful eyeshadow! If you do get transfer smudging, allow it to dry before flicking it away with a cotton bud. Waterproof mascara will stay put whether it's wet weather, a hot day or you're going swimming. Keeping the bulk of your mascara to the root of the lashes and the tips of them feather-light will also help to prevent smudging and flaking.

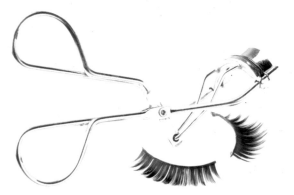

Applying false lashes

I recommend that you line your upper lash line with eyeliner, right into the roots of your lashes, before applying false lashes. This technique allows the natural and false lashes to blend together at the very root so that the false lash line is not apparent. Running a small amount of black eyeliner along the edge of the false lash will hide any tell-tale signs that they are false.

Always measure your falsies against your natural lash line. They should fit exactly from the inner corner (where your natural lashes begin) to the outer corner where the lashes finish – if they don't, you'll need to trim them. Trim from the outer portion of the false lashes, not from the inner, as the inner corner should always have the shortest hairs.

If your lashes are sparse and you can't use this as a guide, ensure that you trim the lashes to start at the beginning of the whites of your eyes and to finish no further than the end of the whites of your eyes. If they go beyond the whites of your eyes it gives a droopy sad effect. The aim with any makeup is always to uplift.

Curl your natural lashes so that the falsies sit well within them. Sometimes, if the lashes are very natural, their edges are comprised of white dots. If this is the case, before removing them from the packet, take a liquid or gel eyeliner and paint over the edge, so that when you put them on the white dots are not visible. This saves you having to try and cover them up once the lashes are on; if you are not wearing eyeliner it's even more essential.

Run a small line of glue along the back of your hand. Now, run the edge of the lash through the glue and add extra to the ends (this is where lashes commonly peel and fall off if there is an insufficient amount of glue). Wait for the glue to become tacky for thirty to sixty seconds – don't worry, you will have plenty of time to move them into the right position, and if you try to stick them on too early then the glue will become messy and you may find the lashes move around.

Holding the lash with a pair of tweezers, place the false lash down onto the centre of your lashes. Now guide the false lash into place from the first natural lash of the inner part of your eye, finishing at the last natural lash of the outer corner of your eye.

Whilst the lashes dry, ensure that you tease them into the right direction. You need to be mindful of the angle that both sets are facing, as you want to avoid one set curling upwards more than the other. Use your fingertips to stroke the lashes downwards and upwards into position whilst they are drying. This will also help the lashes to blend with your own ones to avoid an obvious separation between them. Squeezing the false lashes and your natural lashes together helps to blend them together naturally.

Don't worry if your eyes feel uncomfortable when you first apply the false lashes as they tend to push down on your natural lashes. In order to make them look and feel better, use your mascara, and zigzag through the root of your natural lashes in order to blend them in and lift them up into the falsies.

If you are creating really natural eyes and are not using eyeliner but decide to use false lashes, make sure you check that the lashes you choose have a really thin base. If thick, you will see a black line that looks like eyeliner running along the root of your lash line.

Curling your lashes

Curl your lashes before you apply your mascara. Hold the curler with your thumb and index finger, press and hold at the root for ten seconds. Walk the curler up and hold again, and keep walking the curlers up your lashes until you finish at the tips. This prevents lash creasing and creates a beautiful curve. Don't have a lash curler to hand? Apply a coat of mascara, and whilst it's still wet hold your mascara wand at the root of your lashes, gently pressing upwards for ten seconds, and then zigzag up through them, repeating this until you are satisfied with the curl. Avoid curling your lashes after mascara as it causes the lashes to stick together, and it can also make your lashes brittle.

Shaping beautiful brows

Our eyes are not only the windows to our souls, they are the focal point of our faces. Lots of women either leave their eyebrows out of the makeup equation, or make them too prominent. However, apart from your base, your eyebrows really are one of the most important features on your face. If they are shaped correctly and if the colour is right, your eyebrows frame and lift your face.

If you play around with the colour of your eyebrows it can completely change the way that you look. If they are too dark it can look harsh and ageing, however if they follow your natural colour they are a huge part of enhancing your beauty and keeping your looks youthful. Fierce, block brows with sharp angles can also look particularly ageing, even if you are in your twenties!

Try tidying just one eyebrow first and then see in the mirror how different one side of your face looks to the other. Have a play with an eyebrow pencil and alter the shape; you'll see how different it makes you look!

Notice how much more glamorous and polished your look becomes when your eyebrows are full, in comparison to when they are thinner. Please note – thin eyebrows do not make you look youthful, they actually age you. If you want to mimic a particular look, which involves a different shape, don't pluck them away; just block them out by sweeping concealer through your eyebrows using a dry mascara wand.

Even the most unruly eyebrows on a model are actually styled that way; gorgeous eyebrows really are key to a completed magazine-style transformation.

The perfect shape

Let's not beat around the bush. Rather than showing you what shape your eyebrows shouldn't be, I'm going to show what shape they *should* be.

Ladies, don't be tempted to make your eyebrows thin, leave them at their natural fullness and define their natural shape by plucking, threading or waxing from beneath them, following your natural arch – your natural arch will be the most flattering. Place a pencil against the outer bridge of your nose next to your eyebrow and the middle of your nostril; this will show you where your eyebrows should begin. Previously, beauticians would advise you to place the pencil against the side of your nose, but this causes the eyebrow to be too short.

Next, place the pencil from the bottom of the nose and lean it gently against your lashes in line with the middle of your pupil – this indicates where the arch should begin and will also be the highest point of your natural arch. The arch should finish at the very end of your eye. Place the pencil from the bottom of your nose to the outer corner of your eye. Your brows should form a full, long, elegant curve.

PRO TIP

Mark the beginning, middle and end of your eyebrow with white eyeliner. Next, following your natural curve underneath the brow, connect the dots to draw your perfect shape. Pluck away the stray hairs that fall into and below this white line.

Tidying your brows

- Use a dry mascara wand brush and sweep the hairs upwards and outwards to create your perfect sweeping shape.
- We are taught never to pluck from the top; the most perfect curve should lie beneath them.
- If you have long stray hairs that don't curve with your natural curve, brush the hairs down and trim the ends – but be especially careful not to trim too much. You don't want bald patches!
- If you still have a strong structure to your eyebrows, fill through any gaps with a powder.

● If you have no structure and unruly brows use a pencil or wax. Avoid black- or red-based brow colours at all costs as these are very ageing. Opt for your neutral ashy brown, blonde colours, and use feathery fine lines to give the appearance of real hair – no solid block brows, as harsh, hard-lined brows are also very ageing. Use a felt-tip eyebrow pen to create fake hair for sparse eyebrows. These pens are generally also waterproof and so are a fantastic option for those who have lost their brows because they will not smudge.

HELPFUL HINT

I would recommend using an eye pencil as a guide before using a felt-tip pen because they dry quickly and are more difficult to remove than regular eyebrow pencils.

The desired result is soft, and the strokes should look like natural hairs. Remember that you're catching your natural hairs rather than drawing on your skin. Always start to fill them in a couple of millimetres after they start so that it doesn't look like a solid block. In the same way, follow the bottom of your arch rather than the top – creating too much density at the top will look like you've stuck your eyebrows on.

Use a brow gel to set any product you have used, and to keep any stray hairs in place. It acts like a hairspray, giving you fabulous stay-proof eyebrows for hours.

If you tend to leave your hair uncoloured, and both your eyebrows and hair are grey or white, skip the brow filling in and go straight for the eyebrow gel, sweeping the hairs upwards to set them into a beautiful, gentle arch. If you prefer to colour your eyebrows, having a brow tint treatment with a beautician is an alternative option.

Tinting and lightening your brows the easy way

Only ever tint or lighten your eyebrows with chemical solution if you are a beauty therapist.

If you are a makeup artist working on a shoot, or you want to lighten your own eyebrows, use brow mascara or a concealer instead – you can buy various colours to suit every tone of hair, from blonde to brunette to redhead.

Remember that eyebrows are often darker than the hair on our heads: just because your hair colour is light doesn't mean that your eyebrows have to match it exactly.

Once you have had your eyebrows plucked, waxed or threaded, leave them free from makeup for the rest of the day. When the root of the hair is pulled away it leaves an open pore, which needs to breathe and heal. If you clog it up with product it could cause an infection, or spot.

75

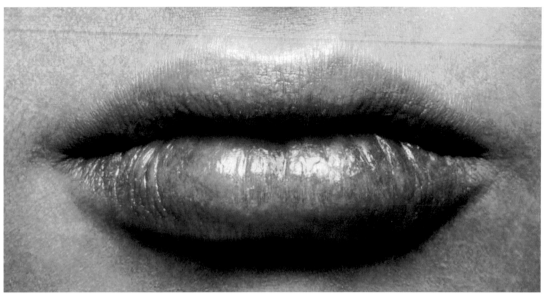

Colouring luscious lips

Lip products

Tinted balm – Tinted balm is a great everyday product because it is easy to apply and nourishing for your lips. It has a very sheer finish, giving just a light hint of colour to the lips; it complements a 'healthy glow' makeup perfectly.

Gloss – Gloss is a perfect way to achieve luscious lips; it gives them a very sensual appearance and has the ability to make thin lips appear fuller. Good quality glosses should not feel sticky; they should feel like more of a smooth balm in texture. Gloss can be worn alone, over lip liner, lipstick or lip tint. Glosses are available in sparkly, metallic, opaque and sheer finishes.

Satin lipstick – Satin lipstick has sheen to it; it feels creamy to apply and gives full coverage. It keeps lips feeling hydrated whilst maintaining strong colour. Perfect for a bold look.

Matte lipstick – Matte lipstick is the ultimate bold lip colour; it really makes a statement because it gives the fullest coverage and often has the strongest pigment (colour) intensity of all of the formulas. I myself prefer satin, as matte colours can appear ageing and dull. If I do use a matte lipstick I will apply it over a balm, unless I am using it for a makeover that needs to look matte.

Matte colour is brilliant when it comes to a red lip, because it stains the lips more, rather than slipping and sliding over the surface, making a mess. If you use a satin lipstick or gloss to achieve a red lip, use a lip liner to fill your lips in slightly first to make it longer-lasting.

Metallic lipstick – Bold in colour, with a glittery or metallic shiny finish.

Lip tint – Lip tint is a brilliant product for staining the lips to achieve a longer-lasting finish. These can be quite drying so I recommend using a balm beneath them.

Any lipstick can be used as a tint, just add it straight to your lips and blot with a tissue to remove most of the product but leave the colour. My favourite trick, however, is simply to press the colour into lips using my finger – it keeps it modern and uncomplicated.

Lip formulas

Hydrating – These are lovely and moisturising.

Plumping – A good option for those who would like fuller lips. I myself find that these don't make a huge difference, although they make the lips 'feel' fuller. I find using a regular lip-gloss just as effective, especially if I sweep it over the edge of the Cupid's bow.

Long-lasting – I'm not a fan of 'longer-lasting formulations'. They can be very drying, and I find it more effective to use a lip tint on your lips followed by a lipstick.

Lip colours

I tend to avoid matte chalky colours because they do nothing to enhance a complexion, whether young or mature. Creamy pastels give a much more flattering finish.

Porcelain skin tones (*the lightest skin tone*)
Look great in soft peachy nudes, cool pinks and soft reds.

Medium skin tones (*Caucasian*)
Look great in peach, coral, warm pinks and warm nudes.

Olive skin tones (*tanned*)
Look great in peach, oranges, gold, bronze, berry and reds with an orange undertone.

Dark skin tones
Look great in oranges, rich reds, vibrant pinks, plums, caramels and browns.

If you have mature skin you should steer away from dark or dull colours that can look ageing and instead opt for vibrant, bright or light colours that complement your complexion.

Lips are a feature that really completes your look. Whether you are opting for a nude or bright lipstick, or even just a glossy finish, your lips need to feel beautiful. Have you ever noticed how it affects your self-esteem when your lips are dry or flaky? This is because our lips make us feel sexy. So much emphasis lies upon our lips – kissing, flirting, drinking, eating, pouting in photos – try not to neglect them!

Whilst on my travels in Australia the importance of lip care became really apparent to me. It being the summer and having to keep well hydrated, I realised just how much my lips needed and I started using a product called Papaw balm. This is a multi-purpose product that is amazing for everything from lips to burns and scars. I think it's important to opt for natural lip products for their protective and conditioning ingredients. Petroleum-based products can create a film over the lips rather than actually nourishing them, and in some cases can increase drying effects. Whether it is winter, summer, spring or autumn, the weather is a constant trigger for dehydration. Many of us also forget about SPF (Sun Protection Filter) on our lips, even though they have the thinnest skin on the face and therefore absorb many UVA and UVB rays.

Use an SPF everyday, whether you pop some of your facial SPF over your lips or whether it is contained within your lip balm. Wear lip balm throughout the daytime and especially at night when we generally don't drink a lot.

Use a lip scrub or a toothbrush that will gently exfoliate your lips once every one or two weeks just to eliminate any dry skin that may be there.

For a softer, 'kiss me' look, apply your lipstick with a fingertip – the warmth of your hands will melt the product into your lips, giving a delicate finish.

For a bright, bold look, apply the colour directly from the tube onto your lips. For a very precise look, like a Hollywood red lip, apply your lip colour using a lip brush.

Using a lip liner is brilliant if you want slightly more definition or a longer-lasting lipstick application. Avoid drawing a solid line around your lips, as when the lipstick wears off, you will be left with only an outline! Instead, use small feathering motions to fill the lips in slightly. That way, as your lipstick disappears you will still be left with colour on the lips. For the most intense colour result, apply your lipstick straight from the tube. If you like to use lip liner to intensify the outline, use a nude shade the same shade as your natural lip colour, or a lip liner that matches your lipstick colour. Highlight your Cupid's bow and directly below the bottom lip to give them a pouty pout.

I find that using a lip brush also helps to make your lipstick last longer because it presses the product into the lips rather than gliding it across them. If you start from the outer corner of your mouth and pull the lip brush in towards the centre of your lips it will give you a solid, straight line. For a softer look, simply use the brush to press the product into the lips. If you apply lipstick directly from the tube ensure that you again press the product into your lips. Gliding it over them may result in a build-up of too much product that will simply slide off – in other words, you are more likely to eat your lipstick than wear it and it is much more likely to feather!

A great pigmented lipstick should give you the colour that you desire in one coat. The fact that there is minimal product on the lips means that it will be far more stay-proof than if you have to apply too many coats that will simply slide one on top of another, causing a mess.

Food for thought …

Imagine how many lipsticks we women eat over one year, wearing it every day … It's pretty horrible, right? We should surely make it good for us!

When I am working with ill patients using makeup therapy, I feel that it is really important to use truly nourishing products on their skin, and to know exactly what is in them.

CHAPTER 4

Learning the Art of Contouring

The key to gorgeous flawless skin is skin that looks completely real and natural. Whether you are contouring, creating a tan or wearing blush it should never be obvious – your makeup should appear airbrushed, flowing from head to chest.

Contouring involves using a mixture of highlight and shadow. Shading naturally creates highlights – like drawing with a black pen on white paper, the light stands out against the dark because it creates a contrast. This technique is used in everyday life to make objects appear three-dimensional; the same rule applies to makeup.

Look at your face and try to visually map out the areas of light and shadow. You will find the highlighted areas are the highest points of your face and those that are in shadow are the features that recede, like just beneath our cheekbones, and within the hollows of our eyes.

I love using creamy contouring products because they blend so easily. Remember to do this after foundation and before powder so that the contouring product glides on and doesn't cake on the skin or cling in patches. If you are wearing powder foundation, use a powder contouring product, again so that it gels well with the skin. The most important aspect of contouring is blending so that you can see absolutely no visible lines, so that it appears like natural shadows within the hollows of your facial structure.

Highlighting

Highlighting products are light-reflective and are a key element in sculpting the face. Used in conjunction with contouring products (which create shadow), they create dimension and definition. I'd always recommend using a highlighter if you have dry skin, or if you are opting for a dewy or sheeny complexion.

Applying highlighter before foundation will give your skin a soft sheen. For intense highlights I apply it once foundation is on.

To create a wet-look, dewy skin (often created by makeup artists for fashion magazine work), mixing foundation with an illuminiser will create a fantastic base. Also, layering a shimmer highlight over a cream one will make it pop.

Absolutely everyone wants radiant skin. Besides an amazing foundation, and fabulous contouring techniques, highlighting creates that celebrity expensive skin.

Highlighting involves 'bringing forward' your features, adding light to the high points of your face where light would naturally fall.

I have oily skin and people often ask me what I have used to highlight my cheekbones. More often than not it's just the sheen of my natural skin through a great liquid foundation.

Because I have oily skin I don't use highlighter unless I want an ultra-dewy complexion, I literally just contour my features, and use powder on the areas that I don't want to shine. If I want a more intense contour, I work with the light and dark technique, which I discuss in the contour section.

HELPFUL HINT
Avoid using white or silver highlighter to highlight beneath your brow bone: it looks unnatural and far too bling. A good rule of thumb is to choose a highlighter with the same tone as your skin – no lighter and no darker – or something translucent.

Test your highlighter along the top of your cheekbone; it should simply create a beautiful sheen – if you can see any colour it is the wrong shade. My favourite highlighting products are creams because I find that they blend into the skin so well they look just like a shine on your skin, whilst powders sometimes appear shimmery and sit more obviously on the skin's surface.

For a dewy shine I would recommend cream or liquid, and for a shimmery, bronzed skin I'd recommend a shimmery powder highlighter or a shimmery cream, only on the tops of the cheekbones and on the eyes. The rest of the face should have non-shimmery highlights for real-looking skin. Too much shimmer all over the face can look unnatural.

There are some fabulous shimmer bricks on the market that contain multiple colours for varying skin tones. If you are going to use a powder highlighter, remember to dust translucent powder over the areas that you want to highlight first, so that it doesn't cling in patches to the foundation beneath it.

To create super intense, catwalk highlights, apply a cream highlighter first, and then dust a powder shimmer over the top of this for a strong reflective finish.

Translucent highlighter suits all, however you can also buy different shades. Here are some examples of what might suit:

– If you have pale skin, you could opt for a very light cream or gold colour highlighter.

– If you have peachy skin, you could opt for a peach or champagne highlighter.

– If you have olive or Asian skin, you could opt for a gold or bronze highlighter.

– If you have black skin with a golden undertone you could opt for a shimmery brown or bronze highlighter.

– If you have a red undertone, you could opt for a shimmery brown or plum highlighter.

For the darkest skin tones highlighting is more effective than contouring, and bringing the cheekbones forward with a bronze shimmer is gorgeous.

If you don't have the correct shade of highlighter, use the highlighter you do have mixed with some of your regular foundation or tinted moisturiser, or even just a regular moisturiser for a translucent glow.

Alternatively, use a highlighting moisturiser beneath or on top of your foundation on the areas that you wish to highlight – perfect for the darkest of skin tones where highlighting is used more than contouring, and where highlighting products can often appear chalky.

Some key things you should keep in mind about highlighting:

- Highlight before you shade when you're working with a cream or liquid highlighting product. I find that if you use highlighter on top of shading it can create patches within your shading when you blend one into the other. Using it the other way around allows the products to blend together seamlessly.

- You can apply highlight with a brush for precision, or use your fingers to blend the product into the skin. Use powder highlight with powder foundation, cream with cream and gloss. If you mix cream highlighter with powder foundation it may become cakey.

Highlight the highest points of your face

You should highlight the highest points on your face:

– The centre of your forehead (between your eyebrows a couple of centimetres up).

– Down the bridge of your nose for the illusion of a straighter, slimmer nose.

– The inner corner of your eyes for the illusion of brightness (although avoid this if you have wide-set eyes as it may make them appear even wider).

It is also lovely to highlight the centre of your eyelid – your makeup will seem three-dimensional and your eyes will look wide awake and sparkly. If you are wearing light eyeshadow, highlight before you apply your eye makeup. If you are wearing dark eyeshadow I'd recommend highlighting your eyelids after you have completed the eye makeup, using a small sweep of shimmer eyeshadow.

> ### HELPFUL HINT
> For super wide-awake eyes, highlight the edge of your nose directly in line with the inner corner of your eyes. Note that if you have wide-set eyes this will make them appear wider – if this is the case, highlight just the outer edge of the tear duct.

You can also highlight:

– Along the top of your cheekbones.

– Across the Cupid's bow (the edge of your upper lip, to make your lips appear fuller).

A light-reflective perfecting pen can also be used beneath dark under eyes for a brightening effect. I like to use this in conjunction with yellow or orange corrector for light and dark skin tones. For help with minimising under-eye darkness completely, see page 43.

Remember that it's not essential to highlight every single area of the face with highlighting product; it really depends on the look you are creating. If you are creating a strong sheen to the face with lots of highlight, then you probably want to opt for highlighting most, if not all, of those areas. However, if you want a soft glow, you can leave some areas naturally highlighted through the use of shading, and highlight other areas with an extra sheen using your product.

If you want to create a soft highlight, use a cream or liquid highlighter on the areas you wish to highlight. Use a fluffy brush to lightly buff over the highlighted areas with your regular foundation, then finish with a light sweep of translucent powder, leaving your skin with a subtle glow. You can also switch your highlighter for an illuminated moisturiser that has a less intense glow/shine.

If you want to create a more intense highlight, highlight once your foundation is done, before using shading or a bronzer, and powder only the areas of your face that you wish not to shine – your T-zone.

Shading

This is an advanced technique, so don't get flustered if you don't grasp it straightaway.

Shading is designed to change and enhance features to give the face a beautiful three-dimensional appearance, and is completely separate from bronzing, although some people get them confused.

Foundation diminishes natural shadow, so it's important to bring warmth and shape back into the face, whether it be with contouring, bronzer, blush or all three.

Use your fingers to feel your bone structure; the shadows should follow the hollows. Your contouring product must always be matte in texture; shimmery products look completely unnatural.

The shadows that fall on our faces are a grey brown colour, not a red brown, so when choosing a contouring shade I recommend using a product with a yellow hue or undertone – unless you have black skin, which is the exception and would require a deep matte brown or a highlighter in its place.

85

The main thing is that any product that you choose for your contouring must be a natural skin tone. If your skin is black you may find highlighting more successful than shading due to contrast of colour.

If you are working with a bronzing product it's really important to keep in mind that you are contouring and not bronzing or creating a tan at this point, you are purely 'shaping' the face.

The products I find most effective are cream or powder contouring products. If you choose to use powder in conjunction with a cream or liquid foundation, ensure that you press translucent powder into the areas of your skin that you wish to contour so that the colour doesn't stick to your base in patches.

Blend everything with a fluffy powder brush so that there are no obvious lines. The result should be skin that tapers gently from light to dark, creating the illusion of shadows.

Whether you are shading using a cream, liquid or powder the techniques that I find most fabulous are identical.

Taking your darker colour for shading and sculpting your face, begin to map out the areas that you want to define.

For very soft contours, use a shade just a few shades darker than your natural skin tone. For more dramatic contours, build the colour up gradually using thin layers.

Always look straight ahead when you are shading so that you can see the shadows occurring.

The darkest areas are always around the perimeter of your face and fade into nothing towards the centre.

Contouring your cheekbones is a fabulous technique for people who wish to achieve those supermodel cheekbones and who want to make their face appear slimmer.

If you have very chiselled cheekbones and a really thin face, go easy on the cheek contouring because if they become too prominent it may make your face appear even thinner.

Keep your contours ultra soft during the day when light is more harsh and unforgiving. You can intensify contours at night when the light is softer.

Use a contouring shade only slightly darker than your overall complexion.

If you choose to shade and not highlight, this should not cause a problem because the contrast of shadows against your skin will create natural highlight within the areas that are not shaded.

PRO TIP

With each area of your face that you contour, take a fluffy powder brush with a fine layer of translucent powder dusted onto it and buff over the areas to blend them into a soft shadow.

Supermodel cheekbones in one minute

I find it easiest to use a fine fan brush to shade beneath the cheekbones. Beginning from the top of your ear, shade beneath the cheekbone (suck your cheeks in and feel where the hollows are), stopping in line with the outer corner of your eyes. Blend over the area with a powder brush to create a soft, graduated shadow.

Opening up your eyes

Look straight ahead into the mirror and apply shadow to where you can see your socket line is. Take a fluffy eyeshadow brush and sweep through your socket line very lightly with the tip of the brush, using a windscreen wiper motion. This keeps the colour soft. This is great to do if you are planning on wearing a 'no makeup look' but still want your eyes to be defined. It's a fantastic technique for really opening up the eyes.

Lifting your eyes

To lift your eyes take your fan brush and contour from the outer corner of your eyes up towards your temples.

Contouring your hairline

This is a great technique for softening a face shape and for making a forehead appear smaller – but if you have an overly small forehead I would not recommend shading your hairline.

Blend the colour around the edge of your forehead right at the hairline. Using your powdered fluffy brush, sweep over the colour from left to right using a windscreen wiper motion; this will taper the colour gradually down the forehead.

Contouring your jawline

Contouring your jawline creates definition, softens a square jaw and also makes a face appear slimmer.

Blend colour around the jawline, blending it slightly down onto the neck so that the colour flows. This has to be blended absolutely seamlessly so that it doesn't look like you are simply wearing the wrong colour foundation! No tide lines, please!

Defining and creating the illusion of a slimmer nose

Shade down both sides and blend, also highlight down the centre (the bridge of your nose), stopping before the tip, for extra definition.

To make a thin nose appear wider: Highlight down the sides and shade down the bridge of the nose.

To make a long nose appear shorter: Highlight down the bridge of the nose and shade the tip.

Defining your lips

Highlight the edge of your Cupid's bow (the dip in your top lip). Define your natural lip line very softly using nude lip liner. Use the pencil to sketch in areas that need definition. Avoid drawing a hard line around the lips.

Either add gloss to your newly lined lips, or blend or pat a small amount of lip-coloured lipstick into your lips with your fingertip.

89

CHAPTER 5

Makeup through the Ages

The most important tip that I can ever give you about makeup for any age is that it should make you look healthy. For younger women, it is simply a way of highlighting your beauty. For older women, it is all of that plus an instant rolling back of the years.

Something I'd love to see more of in the beauty industry is older women promoting makeup brands alongside the younger generation. I understand that the marketing people want to use young beautiful models in anti-ageing campaigns, and that revenue is created when women buy products in the hope of looking like the young beautiful models, but women of all ages love makeup. I am sure that even more women would want to buy products modelled by their age group.

I've spoken to many mature women about the makeup industry, and almost every woman that I speak to feels that there is more emphasis on anti-ageing than anything else, which can make them feel inadequate.

As women age and their faces change they can stumble, 'What colours should I be wearing now?' The colours that we love, adore and know so well suddenly have a big question mark hanging over them: 'Will these colours make me look like mutton dressed as lamb?' Well, why should teens get all the fun? Of course you can still enjoy your favourite colours and styles of makeup! Forget the dusty old compact, today's modern women are loving the trendy brands and are wearing them with style.

Embracing your age

As young adults we bounce through life with a spring in our step. We have a new-found independence and youthful pretty looks. If you are a mature woman you may be thinking, 'What I'd give to look like that again'. Why? I ask. As a mature woman you have a whole new exciting you to explore! I want to help you to recognise, love and make the most of this chapter in your life.

Be confident in who you are
'Inspire and be inspired'

There are makeup articles left, right and centre educating us on 'the latest trends', but remember that each of us has an individual look, style and personality and not every trend needs to be followed. The idea behind everyday makeup is to accentuate your true beauty. Whilst I enjoy following certain fashion trends, I like to make them my own. I liken following trends exactly to the days of wearing school uniform, when everyone had to look the same – where is the personality in that? In a sense, by doing the opposite or adding your own twist on something you stand out – don't hide away, be proud of who you are and let it shine through. I love the quote by Marilyn Monroe, 'Wanting to be someone else is a waste of the person you are.'

I remember as a young girl I'd sit and watch my granny, Jane, a very beautiful women who had been an actress in her youth, and was then an artist, sitting at her dressing table in the morning applying her famous deep coral lipstick. That is still one of the fondest images I have of her. Today, deep coral is still such a dominant colour trend, not just for youth, but for everyone. My granny wore that lipstick with pride until the day that she died, amongst some other vibrant pinks and reds. Never one to shy away, this simple touch of vibrant colour always made her glow. Her makeup was always something that she had just right, the colours she chose made her features pop and her skin look alive, and her makeup was always well moisturised and never thick and drying. I was mesmerised by how beautiful a dash of additional, vibrant colour made her look.

Today, as I look back, I know that those mornings watching her apply her makeup, combined with the days I spent painting with her in her art room, all contributed to my love of makeup as an art being born. One of the most fascinating things that I have learnt over the years is just how much trends go round in circles, simply becoming more advanced and modern with each year.

In much the same way, makeup should grow with us too, as we keep it modern and luscious as each year turns.

Top tips for ageless beauty

Use a moisturising cream, gel or liquid foundation; this should have yellow undertones – never any pink or beige, as they are very unnatural and ageing.

Choose creamy concealers which blend into the skin without settling into lines. Setting your concealer lightly with powder will ensure this further.

Apply your creamy concealer under your eyes and also just under your lips in the crease of your chin. Use it also in the outer corner of your eyes where we get some redness.

Lightening the inner rim of your eyes with a white pencil will eliminate any redness.

Choose an eyeshadow colour that complements your eye colour. If you have green eyes, you could opt for purples, violets or mahogany. If you have blue eyes, you could opt for a bronze gold or brown. I have used a turquoise eyeshadow on model Claire pressed all over the eyelid and blended into her socket line for a modern, simple look. When finding your socket line, keep your eyes open and look straight forward into a mirror. Place your brush in the crease of your eyes and sweep from left to right with the tip of the bristles, using a feather-light touch.

As eyes age the skin droops. A common mistake women make is to apply shadow to the socket line when their eyes are closed. To keep colour within the socket line of your eyes, and avoid going too high towards your eyebrows, apply with your eyes open.

Popping shimmer on the inner corner of your eyes by the tear ducts will instantly brighten them.

If you are using shadow or eyeliner along your lower lash line, keep it very soft. Too much product underneath can drag the eyes down. Touch your brush to the root of your lower lashes to create gentle definition rather than a harsh line. Pushing the liner into the root of your top lashes will give the same effect without a harsh line. It will really open up your eyes and make the lashes look thick and lush.

Curl your lashes before you apply your mascara, as this will really widen, brighten and lift them. Putting lashes onto the outer corner of your lash line will really help to pull your eyes up further.

Lengthening your eyelashes with lash primer will help to prevent mascara smudging down underneath your eyes during the day.

Fill through your eyebrows to keep them looking full, using a colour that either matches your natural brow colour, or is ever so slightly lighter. Avoid using a shade that is too dark as this can be ageing.

Contouring beneath your cheekbones and at the outer corner of your eyes, pulling up towards your temples, will really lift your bone structure. Once your cheeks begin to hollow however, contouring could make you appear gaunt. Instead, stick to blusher and bronzer over the apples of your cheeks. Highlighting your temples can also help to give a thin face a fuller appearance.

Keep blush warm – peaches, apricots and soft coral pinks all flatter mature skin. If your skin has begun to appear more sallow in colour, these shades will really make it pop. Opt for cream blush where possible for a natural youthful radiance. Apply blush to the cushiony apples of your cheeks to give skin back its appearance of plumpness. A small sweep of rose-tinted shimmer across the apples of the cheeks will also give an illusion of a youthful cushiony appearance.

Many women opt for darker lip shades or pale lilac colours as they age, however these can be more ageing and make lips look thin and lifeless. Instead opt for colours that are slightly brighter than your natural lip colour.

Vibrant colours like peaches, corals, bright plums, bright pinks and soft reds are all fantastic and will give your complexion a radiant lift. To test whether a shade is right for you, pop the colour onto your fingertip and hold it up next to your lips. You should see your face light up if you have the right colour.

Your lips need healthy definition. Add moisture to them using a balm or plumping product. Use a nude lip liner to trace definition back into the edge of your lips, using small strokes and working from the outer corner of your mouth inwards. Only focus on the areas that need it — you do not need to draw a line around the entire lip – and blend the product onto your lips so that there are no hard lines.

Apply the lipstick from the outside in, always starting from the outer edges of your lips, as this minimises dragging thin skin and helps to prevent the lipstick from feathering.

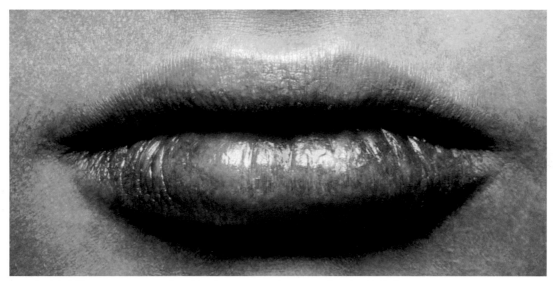

Apply highlighter to your Cupid's bow to make your lips look fuller.

Twenties

To embrace the youthful glow of Emily's skin I chose to keep her makeup very 'girl next door', with a warm glow to her complexion, and cool tones against her green eyes and warm red hair. I teamed this with pretty rose-tinted lips.

First, I swept a slate grey eyeshadow over Emily's eyelids, blending it up into the socket line. The same shadow was taken lightly along the lower lash line.

Emily's upper and lower lash lines were lined with electric blue eyeliner, an everyday take on the neon colours we so often see used on the catwalk. Black mascara was applied to both upper and lower lashes. I kept Emily's skin very sheer and let her stunning freckles shine through (covering freckles looks unnatural and chalky).

I applied a nourishing lip balm to Emily's lips, followed by pressing a rose-tinted lipstick on top of that to create a subtle, natural tint. Emily's eyebrows were tidied with brow wax and set with brow gel.

Thirties

Some of you may already recognise Kate McIntyre as a TV presenter. Kate is a wonderful, lovely and gentle woman, and when she agreed to shoot for the front cover of my book I was so delighted. It was a really fun day and she is a beautiful woman, an asset to my book and a brilliant example of a modern woman, juggling work and home life whilst maintaining a chilled-out attitude. Kate explained to me that they often do their own makeup for documentaries; I thought it would be nice to combine her TV personality, off-stage personality and a pretty playful edge all in one look.

I wanted to reflect her gentle, pretty personality through her makeup. Kate's skin is cool and she has cool blue eyes, so I opted for a silver cream eyeshadow that would enhance this. I defined her upper lash line with fine black eyeliner and black mascara. I lined her lower lash line with the silver cream eyeshadow to keep her eyes soft. Kate's brows were tidied with brow gel – they are naturally full and I wanted to keep them that way without making them any darker because her natural hair colour is lovely and light. To keep the overall look warm, I opted for peachy pink blusher on the apples of her cheeks and swept up to the highest point of her cheekbones. I then finished the look with a glossy peachy pink lip.

Forties

Claire has beautiful hazel eyes, and I wanted to keep the look very natural and warm so opted for bronze eyes and nude lips with a gentle flush of a sun-kissed glow through the complexion.

I applied a creamy foundation to Claire's skin, mixing light with dark to complement her warm skin tone. I then warmed the skin further with a bronze-based bronzer and a sweep of peach blush over the cheekbones. Claire's cheekbones are high, so I swept the blush high over her cheekbones, up towards her hairline and then down towards the outer corner of her nose, stopping a thumb's width away from it. This left a triangle of highlight on the cheek from the outer corner of her nose to the outer corner of her eye and then back to the inner corner of her eye. This emphasised her beautifully defined face shape.

I applied a simple bronze shadow to Claire's lower eyelids, blended it into the socket line and softly lined the upper lash line; I kept the lower lash line free from colour to keep the look fresh. Black mascara was then applied.

The look was completed by applying a nude lip liner in a sketchy motion to fill in the lips and define their fullness, with a nude lipstick applied over the top of this, and a final layer of nourishing lip balm.

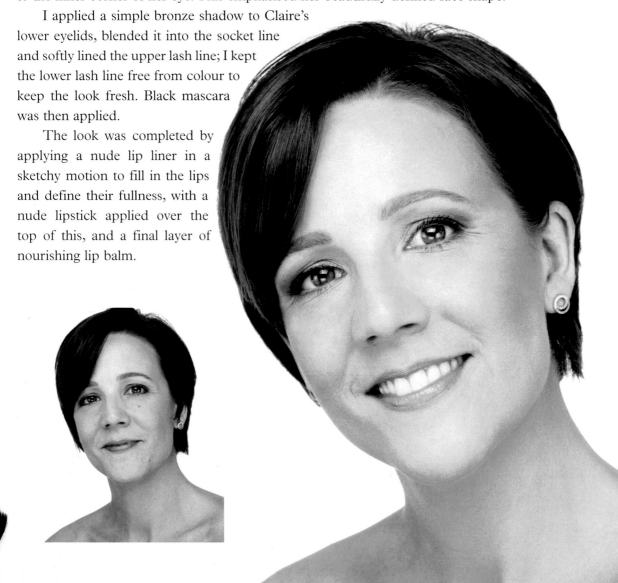

Fifties

Jane has a gorgeous, modern sense of style, which I wanted to reflect in her makeup. I took her current day makeup, which uses soft purple eyeshadow, and created purple smoky eyes, which complement her hazel eye colour and blue shirt. I teamed that with pink nouveau lips, which set off the pretty finish of her jewellery. Cheeks were kept very neutral, with just a hint of peachy pink blush.

A fine line of dark shadow smudged around Jane's eyes gave them great definition and to finalise her look, I applied a couple of coats of black mascara.

Sixties

This is Anjali's mother Pam, and although they have some very similar features, their overall colouring is opposite. Anjali has a complexion typical of an Asian skin tone, and deep chocolate button brown eyes. Pam has a fair complexion, with piercing baby blue eyes. Together, they are a beautiful contrast to one another.

I kept Pam's makeup light against her dark clothing; I swept a light silver wash all over her eyelids up into the crease and slightly beyond. Black eyeliner really makes blue eyes pop, so I lined the upper lash line with black gel liner and the lower lash line with a black kohl liner. Always smudge liner along the lash line so that it doesn't look too harsh. I prefer to take liner towards the inner corner of the eye rather than stopping halfway because I find that it more clearly defines the eye. I kept Pam's skin looking well moisturised with a hydrating foundation primer and gel foundation blended generously into the skin. I concealed around the nose area, where there is often a certain amount of redness, and brightened the under-eye area. A brow wax was swept through Pam's eyebrows and set into place with a brow gel. The look was completed with a youthful, modern, glossy peach lipstick.

Seventies

Claire was such a beautiful model to work with, full of vibrant personality and features that light up as she smiles. I kept the emphasis with this look on her gorgeous smile and on creating a warm complexion. The soft mauve tones within the grey eyeshadow make her brown eyes sparkle.

To define the shape of Claire's eyes I applied fine dark eyeliner to her top and bottom lashes, pushing the product into the root of the lashes as I went to give the illusion of fuller lashes. Claire's hair colour is such a pretty silver that I didn't want to make her eyebrows any darker, so I simply swept brow gel through them to tidy them and set them in place. The soft red lips set off the peach tones of her blusher and the overall look is warm and friendly.

CHAPTER 6

Creating a Naturally Beautiful You

The idea behind natural, 'barely there' makeup is that it should leave you looking beautifully healthy and radiant without making it obvious that you're wearing makeup at all. I believe that every person on this planet is beautiful; it's just about pinpointing your favourite features and subtly enhancing them. Makeup can work miracles with the way you feel. I do regular work with women who are going through cancer and terminal illness. It is an indescribable feeling seeing these women light up inside as they gaze into the mirror and feel that they look like themselves again.

- Transform tired, sallow skin into skin that looks full of natural health and moisture. Apply a lightweight hydrating moisturiser to the skin followed by a lightweight hydrating foundation.

- Conceal blemishes and any redness around the nose with a creamy moisturising concealer.

- Using your fingertip pat a small amount of eye cream below your eyes just along the very top of your cheekbones. Pat some light-reflective corrector and some regular concealer beneath your eyes.

- Set your skin with face powder.

- Apply blusher to the apples of your cheeks. Beautifully emphasising the fleshy part of the apples of your cheeks can give the entire face a flush of health.

- Next, sweep bronze over the high points of your face (cheeks, the bridge of your nose, forehead, chin and neck). Use a clean powder brush and buff it over your skin to blend it seamlessly.

- Apply a light eyeshadow to your eyelids, followed by a medium shade with a pearly finish. Take a deeper shade and blend it through the socket line.

- Apply mascara from the root to the tips of your upper and lower lashes; keep most of the product to the roots to keep the ends fluttery and natural.

- Define your brows.

- Give your lips a healthy pop of colour using a pink, soft red or berry shade of lipstick.

CHAPTER 7

Wedding Makeup Tips

Bridal makeup

Spring, summer, autumn, winter – bridal season falls all year round, and whether you are opting to do your own makeup, are having a professional do it for you, or it is you who will be doing it for someone else, we all want to know how to achieve that perfect, stay-proof makeup for one of the biggest and most special days of a woman's life. The focus and top priority must be about the bride enjoying her day, so I have put together some tips and a beautiful bridal look, which can suit all year round.

Using the timeless eyeshadow application of three shades to sculpt the eye socket is a classic way of creating a bridal look that will not date. You can have fun with this too, because you can adapt the shape of the sculpting to suit you. The easiest tip for a flattering shape is to follow the shape of the socket line. Every person's eye shape varies, so this is a fail-safe way of achieving a perfect shape. You can also create a smoky eye, a more natural eye, or even change the shape slightly to lift them, make them bigger or make them less pronounced by using more or less product and changing the shape of it slightly. This may mean winging the eyeshadow out to elongate the eyes, sweeping eyeshadow in towards the inner corner of the eye to make wide-set eyes closer, or keeping it lighter for close-set eyes to give the appearance of space between the eyes.

It is important to wear the look that most suits you and that you feel reflects your personality. One look doesn't have to suit all. You can adapt colours, intensity and coverage as you desire. The classic look is simply about defining your features elegantly to really emphasise their beauty to maximum effect.

Be aware that if you choose an on-trend makeup look, you may be disappointed when, in the future, you look back on the photos and your makeup appears dated as that particular trend is long gone. Of course, there is no issue with this if you are aware and comfortable. If you feel that you may look back and scream, 'Ahhh, what was I wearing?', then you may want to have a rethink of your overall look. These photos are your memories for life. Love the day, live the day and capture your greatest memories, whichever look you choose from makeup and hair to dress, shoes and jewellery. You will look back with a smile, knowing it was one of the happiest days of your life.

Some people love going for a dramatic change on their wedding day, but the majority prefer to look like an enhanced version of themselves, particularly so that their husband-to-be recognises them at the end of the aisle! If there are certain things you never go without, like eyeliner, incorporate them into your look.

Keep in mind the colour scheme of your wedding. For example, if you have opted for cool tones – pinks, purples, blues – it would be flattering to follow a similar cool tone throughout your makeup. If your colour scheme is warmer – oranges, corals, golds and yellows – you could choose makeup colours which are warmer and will complement your entire colour scheme. Take note that you can buy various shades of each colour – there are usually neutral versions if, for example, you don't suit completely cool blue undertones, or completely warm red undertones.

If your colour scheme is neutral or monochrome, you can go either way within the colour spectrum for your makeup.

Build the makeup in thin layers and really work them into the skin. This helps to keep it looking natural. People's faces differ hugely in terms of how much makeup looks too much. I find that sometimes, you can literally touch the brush to someone's skin and it's enough, whilst other people's faces seem to absorb the makeup and they can wear much more. Building your colours slowly will prevent you from overloading. Thin layers also help to make the makeup long-lasting, whereas heavy layers tend to slip and slide over one another. There should be nothing left sitting visibly on top of the skin. I always say, neutral tones look great blended seamlessly into the skin for natural emphasis, whilst colour, shimmer and metallics are made to be seen. Foundation is skin-toned for a reason – it is meant to be invisible!

If you are getting married in white, wearing a white top when you trial your makeup really helps to emphasise just how your makeup will look on the day. For example, if you are someone who usually likes to wear lots of fake tan, you may find that against the white it looks even brighter and making it lighter than usual will be more appropriate for your big day. Or you may find that white makes you look a little washed out, in which case you might want to go warmer. It will be easier for you to determine whether to go cooler or warmer with the makeup when you can see what does or doesn't work against the white. You will also need to take into account your natural skin tone here – cool tones will usually look more flattering in cool colours, whilst warm tones usually look more flattering in warm. There are some more neutral skin tones (a mix of both) that can go either way. And of course, there is the fail-safe option of going for neutral tones. Mahogany, for example, is a neutral tone; it contains both red and blue undertones.

You should also take photography into account. People often think that because a photographer is involved, makeup needs to be much heavier than it usually would be, but this is a misconception. In fact I find it couldn't be further from the truth. Bridal makeup is totally separate to studio makeup, because the heavy lighting that diffuses makeup in studio environments doesn't come into play at a wedding.

Wedding photos are most commonly taken in natural daylight, or natural evening light, which is incredibly soft in comparison to studio lights. Even small amounts of makeup are completely visible, and too much can look heavy and unnatural. I was once told by a photographer that he often struggles with this at weddings, because natural lighting can be so unforgiving: dark smoky eyes, for example, look even darker on camera, thus the bride's eyes can become lost. My best advice is to keep eye makeup light and bright, and if you are going smoky, maybe choose shades with a sheen to them that will catch the light and emphasise the shape of your eyes. Keeping your shapes classically beautiful – well blended and feline – and eyeliner soft, will work well in your photographs.

The next thing to think about with photography is shine, shimmer and sparkle control. Flash lighting is regularly used, especially at night, which picks up shine in all the right or wrong places. You can control this by adding the correct amount of highlight to the correct areas yourself, and avoiding unwanted shine.

If you want to add sparkle or shimmer to the makeup, remember to choose your key areas carefully – I recommend no more than two, otherwise it becomes overpowering. If you like the glow look, mix between sparkly eyes and sheeny highlights rather than shimmer everywhere.

Pop the highlighter just on the high points of your face – the tops of the cheekbones looks most beautiful – and really sculpt your cheekbones for a high, slim finish. A small amount of highlighter also looks great on the tops of the shoulders and the collarbones, giving a polished, healthy finish to the skin. Try to avoid shimmer all over the body though, as this may look overpowering and shiny in photos.

When you trial your makeup, take a photo with the flash on to test how your foundation looks. Some foundations contain SPF, and whilst chemical SPFs aren't too much of a problem, SPFs which contain titanium dioxide and/or zinc oxide can make the foundation appear to have a white hue in photographs, making your face look much paler than it does to the naked eye. Too much light-reflective ingredient can also add to this, so stick to formulas which contain just a small amount of light-reflective ingredient. I love oil-free gel formulas for bridal makeup. They are long-lasting, sheer and buildable, they let your natural skin tone come through and give an overall radiant finish. If you do need to wear SPF, or an SPF foundation, counteract the white hue using a coloured powder (the opposite of translucent) and press it into the skin using a powder puff. When choosing powder, I would recommend avoiding HD powders, originally designed for television, as in some cases these have also been linked to white flashback.

Long-lasting makeup is key, so opt for waterproof where possible – for example, eyeliner and mascara. There are also some fabulous long-lasting cream eyeshadows and blushers. If you are using powders, always prime your skin with an oil-free foundation primer (my favourites are the serums, which feel delicious) and use eyeshadow primer, which eliminates any redness and allows the shadow to sit crease-free all day.

Keep in mind that generally you will want to use cream with cream, and powder with powder, to prevent makeup from caking. If you do use cream and powder together, be sure to use the cream first and dust a fine layer of translucent powder between layers, so that one glides onto the other.

Bridal makeup needs to be ultra clean, fresh and flawless. If you start with the eyes, you don't need to worry about shadow falling onto the skin and making it look muddy and having to redo it. You can simply cleanse and wipe away any access once the eye makeup is finished and then begin the foundation. Leave covering under-eye darkness until last also.

When doing your foundation, think about where else your skin is on display. If there are any areas of redness or blemishes that need covering, these can be evened out with your foundation or concealer. Remember to set this with powder, and avoid any areas of skin that will touch or rub against the dress.

My brides often ask me, will my lipstick last all day or do I need to take one with me? I would always recommend taking one. You will be kissing, eating and drinking and lipstick will simply fade over the duration of the day. I would also recommend taking some translucent powder in case you want to freshen up – there will more than likely be lots of dancing! You could ask one of your bridesmaids to pack a small touch-up kit for you, or carry small compact versions in a handbag.

Invariably, brides either opt to do their own wedding day makeup, or they hire a professional makeup artist to do it for them, which allows them to relax and unwind on the day. If you decide to hire an artist, I recommend organising a trial makeup run before the big day, to ensure that you achieve your desired look. The key to your makeup artist achieving what you desire is for them to really listen. When I work with a bride, I begin the consultation by asking them what their vision for their makeup might be. I then find it helpful to see photos of how they would normally do their own makeup, so that I can include any key aspects that apply to them personally. The majority of brides that I work with want to look like they normally would, but a really beautifully polished version, an airbrushed version. The aim is for the bridal party to look utterly beautiful, without really being able to tell that they are wearing lots of makeup.

Using the three-shade eyeshadow approach (light, medium, dark), I created a beautiful classic eye (a classic shape means following the eye's natural shape creating soft, natural definition much like a shadow) in chocolate gold that complements Lucie's deep brown eyes, golden blonde hair and pale peachy skin perfectly. I teamed that with a warm, fresh, rosy complexion and pretty pink lips.

I prepped Lucie's eyes with eyeshadow primer to ensure that her eyelids were even in colour, and to prevent the eyeshadow from wearing off or creasing.

I then applied a light golden-toned eyeshadow, similar to her skin tone, all over her eyelids stopping at the socket line, for natural definition.

I love to see a slight sparkle to bridal makeup, so I opted for shimmery shades. With a small brush I began to pat a chocolate shade into the outer corners of Lucie's eyelids, bringing it up into the socket line and keeping it to the outer portion of her eyes.

To create bigger, more elongated eyes for Lucie, I chose to take the shadowing just above the socket line, keeping it to the outer portion of her eyes. I also elongated it slightly at the sides. I kept quite a definite shape to the eyeshadow, but softened it at the edges using a fluffy blending brush to allow it to blend seamlessly into the skin without any hard, obvious edges – bridal makeup should always be soft.

I ran a darker shade of eyeshadow along the upper lash line from the outer to the inner corner, making sure I pushed it into the lash line so there were no gaps between the root of the lashes and the eyeliner. I ran the same eyeshadow along her lower lash line, stopping about halfway.

I softened the liner using a small sponge brush to smudge the lightest shade over the top of the eyeliner, so it gave soft definition rather than a hard line. I then swept the light shade along the lower lash line to soften that, this time running the brush all the way along to define the rest of the eye very subtly.

To define the brow shape I swept a very light shade beneath the brow bone to highlight the shape. (Use a yellow based shade, not a white one as this will look most natural.)

I then applied additional sparkle to the centre of Lucie's eyelids. I lightly pressed highlighter into the inner corner of Lucie's eyes by her tear ducts, to make her eyes sparkle.

I ran beige eyeliner along the inner rim (waterline) of Lucie's lower lash line to make her eyes look brighter. (Remember, beige looks more natural than white.)

I curled Lucie's lashes and applied mascara top and bottom, wiggling the wand from root to tip.

I added very natural strip lashes to Lucie's eyes from inner to outer corner, and swept a final layer of mascara through her lashes at the roots to lift the real ones and blend them upwards naturally into her false ones. (The weight of lashes sometimes causes your natural lashes to drop, lifting them makes the false lashes feel more comfortable.)

To keep Lucie's eyebrows full and beautiful, I swept them upwards and outwards with a clean dry mascara wand, defining their perfect arch. I then added soft definition with a blonde wax one shade lighter than Lucie's natural brow hairs, running an angled brush through them for precision, using soft feathery strokes to create realistic hair rather than block brows.

Skin

I first used a light cleanser to remove any eyeshadow that had dropped down onto Lucie's skin, and cleansed the rest of her skin to remove excess oil.

Lucie's skin has a natural shine, so I skipped moisturiser and prepped her skin with an oil-free primer, massaging it into her skin in circular motions – both relaxing and great for circulation – to create an ultra-smooth base for her foundation to glide on to, to minimise the appearance of pores and oil, and to help maintain a long-lasting base.

I then applied a long-lasting gel foundation to Lucie's skin, mixing light and dark to create her perfect shade, ensuring the colour matched her entire body. I buffed it into her skin using a multi-use brush, concentrating on the areas that needed it most and keeping it sheer towards the perimeter of her face for a natural, seamless finish.

I covered any blemishes using a non-light reflective concealer with a thick consistency.

117

I popped highlighter onto the tops of Lucie's cheekbones for a subtle sheen and massaged cream blusher into the apples of her cheeks, blending and fading it up towards the temples for a radiant healthy complexion, building the colour up in very fine layers. (Remember that thick layers on top of each other slip, slide and cake.)

I then dusted some translucent powder lightly over her blusher to allow the powder blush to sit perfectly – without clinging and sitting on the surface. For an extra pop of colour, I gently buffed a slightly more vibrant powder blush, with a tiny bit of shimmer for three dimensions, over the apples of Lucie's cheeks in a circular motion. This gave her skin a healthy luminosity without picking up too much shine.

Next, I applied an under-eye pen with some light reflection, but not too much, beneath Lucie's eyes and slightly into the inner corner of her eyes for wide-awake brightness. I worked this into her skin with a little regular concealer for more coverage, keeping it very light and well blended so as not to crease.

Then, I used a non-light reflective powder to set Lucie's base, choosing a translucent powder because its colourless finish wouldn't change the colour of the foundation. I swept a really fine layer over her skin, using circular motions to work it in. I finished by sweeping the brush beneath her eyes, to set the under-eye concealer using only what was left on the brush to prevent it from creasing.

Lips

I applied a small amount of lip balm to Lucie's lips and allowed that to soak in for a couple of minutes (you could apply this before you do the foundation to give it more absorption time). I then lined her lips with a colourless nude pencil to define them and prevent her lipstick feathering. Colourless is great because it won't alter the colour of the lipstick, but if you want definition of the lip line, opt for a coloured nude pencil.

I followed the lip line exactly and filled the lips in lightly. I finished with a moisturising sheer pink lipstick, pressing it into Lucie's lips with a lip brush for precision and to create staying power by working the product into the lips. (If you apply it straight from the tube you tend to get too much product, which will then slip.)

Makeup for bridesmaids

The look of the bridesmaids is largely the decision of the bride and her vision of how she would like them to look. It is important to let the bride make these decisions if she wants to. Some brides have definite ideas of how exactly they would like the makeup to look, other brides allow bridesmaids free reign to wear it how they would like it. In this case the makeup artist should advise what colours and techniques might complement the bride's makeup. Very often the bridesmaids will wear makeup similar to the bride's, and I am sometimes asked to create a more muted version of the bride's makeup for the bridesmaids. Even if you choose to do exactly the same makeup on the bride

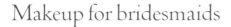

and the bridesmaids, it will look slightly different on each person, because each one is a unique individual with different features and skin tones. Plus, once the bride has her dress on and hair done, she instantly becomes the shining star of the day.

My mother, Christine, is wearing the bridesmaid look featured in this section. She has beautiful big eyes, perfect for showing off eye makeup. Glitter looks great at every age, so I applied a very fine glitter and turquoise eyeshadow to her eyelids to complement both her dress, and her fair skin tone.

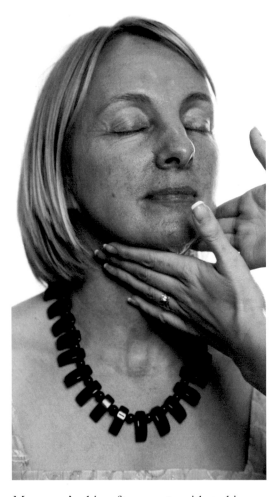

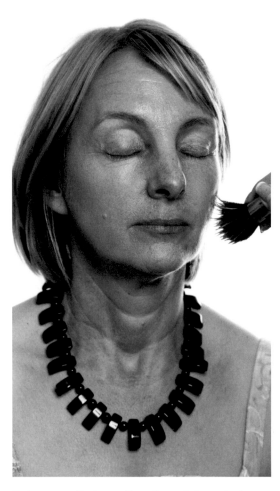

My mum's skin often reacts with a skin condition called rosacea (reddening of the skin which can be triggered by perfumed products). To begin with, I used a soothing moisturiser.

I then applied a yellow-based foundation to her skin, which would counteract the redness and create an even skin tone.

I popped a dusty pink blusher onto the apples of Mum's cheeks to give her complexion a healthy, girlie glow.

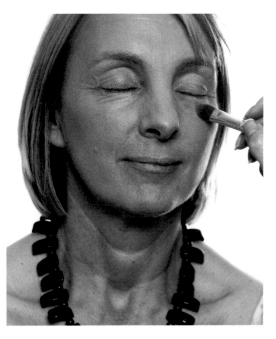

I powdered the skin and ensured any under-eye darkness was lightened and brightened.

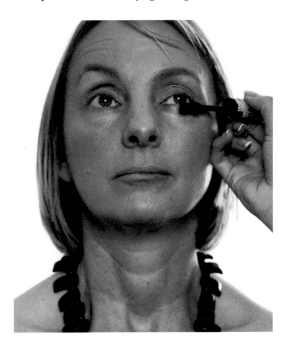

Mascara was applied to the upper and lower lash line.

A baby pink lipstick really complemented Mum's fair skin tone.

121

Makeup for the mature bride

The mature bride looks equally as stunning as a bride in her youth; makeup should be simple, striking, hydrating and radiant. The key focus here is skin – the skin must be flawless and the trick is to recreate the flush of youthful colour that we have when we are young. Mature brides often explain to me that whilst they want to look beautiful, they also want to look sophisticated, so it is important to execute this within the makeup, keeping it fresh and modern, but sophisticated and subtle at the same time.

Step one

One week before the wedding exfoliate your skin with a very gentle face exfoliant to remove any dead skin cells that could cause makeup to become cakey. This will give you a smooth canvas ready for your big day. A facial is a brilliant and relaxing alternative that will leave your skin looking bright and rejuvenated.

Step two

Moisturise your skin with a hydrating moisturiser.

Step three

It is really important to use a thin layer of foundation primer – serum or cream – and massage it well into your skin. Use circular motions with your fingers to pump up your circulation and make your skin glow.

Step four

Using a fluffy fibre-optic foundation brush, buff a hydrating, long-lasting foundation (sheer coverage) into your skin, applying it in very thin layers and building the coverage up in areas that you feel need more. Apply a hydrating eye serum beneath your eyes. Buff the foundation very gently beneath your eyes, and over the eyelids. Using a creamy concealer, buff gently over any areas of darkness using the minimum amount of product – too much product may emphasise lines and may cake and look dry. You can lift extra-dark areas with a small amount of peach corrector followed by your foundation lightly to bring the colour back to your natural skin tone.

123

Step five
Blend a vibrant berry pink or apricot blusher over the apples of your cheeks and high up on the tops of your cheekbones. Powder your skin lightly with a translucent powder.

Step six
Sweep bronzer lightly over your cheeks, forehead, nose, chin and neck ensuring that all edges are blended seamlessly. Sweep a tiny amount of vibrant pink blusher over the apples of your cheeks for an extra vibrant pop of colour to really give the skin a healthy, radiant lift.

Step seven
Apply an eye primer to your eyelids. Press a soft silver coloured eyeshadow all over your lower eyelids and blend into the socket line. Sweep a pearly matte dark grey eyeshadow into the socket line with a fluffy blending brush, focusing on the outer corners of the eyes to add more depth and definition. Look straight forward into your mirror, place the eyeshadow brush in the outer corner of your socket line (the dip or hollow) and sweep the brush around the contour of your eye towards the bridge of your nose. Now move the brush backward and forward in a windscreen wiper motion. This will subtly define the shape of your eyes and lift your eyelids.

Step eight

Apply dark black or grey eyeliner to the root of your upper lash line, and very softly along the lower lash line to enhance and define your eye shape. Curl your lashes and apply black mascara from the root to the tip of your eyelashes, wiggling your wand as you comb through them to keep them separated and avoid clumping.

Step nine

Using an angled eyebrow brush and a soft wax brow definer, use feather-like strokes to gently fill through sparse eyebrows and create a beautiful sweeping brow.

Step ten

Complete the look by sketching over your lips with a neutral lip liner, filling the lips in gently to avoid any hard lines. Press a pink lipstick into your lips and finish with a coat of balm or lip-gloss (glossy or shimmery).

Makeup for the mother of the bride

Makeup can be almost as important a part of the wedding day for the mother of the bride as it is for the bride. Not only do you want to look your best, it is also a chance for you to relax and de-stress and de-fluster with a little pampering. When I asked my mother for her recollections of my own wedding day, she said not only did the makeup give her great confidence, but it was also lovely to get the occasional compliment of 'I can't believe you are her mother, you look so young!', or 'Oh yes, I can tell that you are the mother of the beautiful bride'. My mother explained, as do many mothers of the bride, that she just wanted to look effortlessly natural and elegant.

The key tip for flawlessly elegant mother of the bride makeup is to have it looking well moisturised, soft and radiantly healthy. Colour should pop against your skin adding that youthful glow. Don't be afraid to use a little sparkle or shimmer on your eyes – women are often told to steer away from it for fear of enhancing wrinkles, however, if you keep shimmery, metallic or sparkly products to your lower eyelid, they look beautiful, open up the eyes and give them the sparkle they deserve on such a special day. Keeping the socket line matte will tie it all together. Eyeliner really does enhance eyes as you grow older as it lifts and opens the eyes, giving them a wide-awake, bright appearance.

Moisturise skin well before you apply foundation to keep the skin soft and elasticised. Opt for a sheer coverage, hydrating foundation with a silk-like finish. Keep blusher high up on the cheekbones and blend it out over the apples of your cheeks for instant youth. I find that using cream blusher is most flattering because it blends beautifully into the skin and keeps cheeks looking well hydrated and healthy. For an added radiant boost to your complexion, take a light sweep of rose-tinted shimmer over the apples of your cheeks. Choose vibrant, deep colours like berry pinks and apricots – the aim is to recreate the flush of colour that you have shining from within the skin throughout youth. Take a similar approach with your lipstick: berry pinks look amazing and gloss or balm adds health. Shimmer gloss also looks fabulous because again it adds a sparkle to your complexion.

Defined eyebrows instantly lift the face. Often as we age our hair becomes thinner and therefore our eyebrows can lose their definition. Sweeping through them with a soft brow wax gently and subtly defines them. Opt for a natural colour that isn't too dark – dark, solid eyebrows can be incredibly ageing. Feather-like strokes keep brows looking real and elegant.

Neutrals are naturally beautiful. Adding colour to your eyes can be equally beautiful. Here, on model Sarah, I swept a shimmery, vibrant pink eyeshadow over her lower eyelids and in towards the inner corner of her eyes next to the tear ducts to enhance the sparkle of her eyes. I then swept a purple eyeshadow through the socket line for definition, ensuring that I didn't take the colour too high in order to keep it elegant and subtle. To balance Sarah's eyes against her lovely full brows, I ran dark eyeliner along her top lash line and applied false lashes. I kept her lower lash line bare so that the eyes stayed soft and feminine and didn't become too dramatic. To complement Sarah's peachy pink jacket and cream pearls, I applied a soft pink-peach lipstick with a creamy texture to add a gentle shine. This ensured that the lips looked nourished and more neutral than her eyes, keeping the eyes the focus but allowing her beautiful, sparkly smile to dazzle.

CHAPTER 8

Makeup for Busy Mums

Being a mum of two – Lara is six and Megan is just six months – I completely appreciate how frantically busy life can be. Applying your makeup doesn't seem like much of a priority anymore, and often mums can begin to lose themselves. Women often say to me, 'Wow, I'd have to be up at 5.30 to look like this every day!' Not at all. As unbelievable as this may sound, once you have mastered the art of an express make-over you will find yourself applying it in as little as five minutes! If you find this hard to believe, check out my YouTube videos at www.youtube.com/user/EmilyRoseMakeupTV. I have Megan either on my lap or in a harness in a few of them! I feature both of my daughters in a couple of them too.

I have found one of the easiest ways to still manage to enjoy getting ready, or at least to actually achieve getting ready, is to get the kids involved. It's amazing how intently a small baby will watch and learn, and Lara, my eldest daughter, just loves getting involved. She once said to me, 'Mummy, I want to be on YouTube like those other kids', so we sat down and made a video of her applying my makeup and training to be a makeup artist. She loved it!

I've chosen a beautifully bronzed makeup with Gemma's look, which complements her golden skin tone perfectly. This is a look that you could achieve in time to have the kids in bed and head out with the girls!

Step-by-step images

I began by prepping Gemma's skin with a
lightweight moisturiser and serum primer. If
you massage it into your skin you will have a
lovely mini facial prior to makeup application,
which will make your skin glow beautifully.

Gemma has sparse lashes so we opted to
apply false lashes at the beginning of the
make-over. Looking down whilst you apply
them, rather than closing your eyes, will
ensure that your upper and lower lashes
don't get stuck together!

Gemma has a beautiful, even complexion. I applied a sheer golden-toned, long-lasting gel foundation to her skin using a flat foundation brush and using a gentle painting motion to apply it and press it into her skin. I focused the coverage mainly on the centre of her face to enhance the radiance of her skin. The foundation was blended towards the perimeter of her face so that it became invisible.

A yellow-based corrector was applied to the under-eye area to brighten it, followed by a small amount of concealer to blend it to her natural skin tone and provide extra coverage.

Under-eye concealer was set with a light sweep of face powder using a fluffy eyeshadow brush.

131

Using a big fluffy powder brush I reduced any overly shiny areas on Gemma's face – the T-zone is the most common area for shininess. The powder also helped to set her foundation to create a longer-lasting base.

I applied bronzer to the high points of Gemma's face (forehead, nose, chin, tops of cheekbones and neck and collar bones). I then applied a shimmer bronzer over the tops of her cheekbones to enhance the bronzed glow.

To give Gemma's complexion a healthy glow, I applied a pop of vibrant colour to the apples of her cheeks. I chose a deep orange red to complement her golden skin tone.

I applied concealer to Gemma's eyelids to provide a longer-lasting base for her eyeshadow and to prevent it from creasing. You could also use an eye primer in its place. Using a flat eyeshadow brush, I pressed a shimmery gold eyeshadow all over Gemma's lower eyelid.

Taking a fluffy eyeshadow brush I began to blend a medium bronze shade into the socket line of Gemma's eyes and down into the gold eyeshadow. I then took a smaller eyeshadow brush and applied a deeper shade of brown to the outer corners of her eyelids and used the fluffy brush to taper this into the rest of the eyeshadow.

I lined the upper and lower lash line using a flat push brush and a dark chocolate pressed eyeshadow (you could use a wet brush, or an eyeshadow transformer liquid for a more intense line). I then used a smaller brush to soften these lines.

I finished Gemma's look with a berry lipstick and some creamy gloss to enhance her full lips.

134

For a super quick day makeup, moisturise, then massage a sheer foundation into your skin. Apply cream blush to the apples of your cheeks, a slick of mascara to your upper and lower lashes, define your brows with a brow defining product and finish with a sheer tinted lip-gloss or lip balm.

CHAPTER 9

Express Makeup

Glitzy glam

I love glitter, either worn softly during the daytime or more boldly at night. It is fun and eye-catching. If you pop a couple of small flakes just onto the inner corners of your eyes, it gives them that little bright twinkle that everyone so desires, and it's a fun alternative to using shimmer or highlighter there.

This look is super quick and easy to achieve. I recommend starting with your eyes and doing your foundation afterwards so that you can easily wipe away any loose glitter that may fall onto your skin. A good trick for removing hard-to-budge glitter from the skin is to use a piece of sticky tape.

I chose to go strong and glittery with Bridget's eyes to complement her glitzy necklace. The warm tones of the deep orange lipstick contrast against the cool silver tones beautifully.

To achieve this look, simply coat your eyelid in a glitter gel pen. Using your fingertip dab the product to move it around evenly over the eyelid and press loose glitter over the top for extra density.

To finish the look, put a hint of orangey peach blush on the apples of your cheeks and apply a deep orange, coral, or orange-based red lipstick to your lips. For those of you who prefer to wear cool lipstick colours like vibrant pinks or blue-based reds, this will look beautiful.

For a softer daytime look you could use the glitter gel pen on its own. Simply apply it to your upper lash line as you would eyeliner and press it over the eyelid with your fingertip. Finish with a peachy coral or pink lipstick.

Another fantastic way of achieving a glittery eye is to apply a cream shadow base all over your eyelid and press glitter onto this. This is particularly nice if you use a metallic, shimmer, or pearl cream eyeshadow as I have here with a gold cream base and gold glitter. Take it up to the socket line and stop there so that it looks soft and pretty without being too overpowering.

At the office

As a representative of the company you work for, whether it is your own business, a small company, a large company, and whether you are a face of the business or work behind the scenes, a smart appearance is a key attribute. Makeup has immense power to sell. If we look at the beauty industry, for example, people often base their purchases upon how the sales person has done their makeup. Air hostesses are trained specifically to apply beautiful makeup, because they lead the customer experience throughout the flight. Harsh makeup can often give a false illusion of a person's true personality; it can in some cases make them seem less approachable. Soft, pretty makeup often has the opposite effect.

I chose neutral colours that would enhance Marija's green eyes and warm hair colour to complement her soft features.

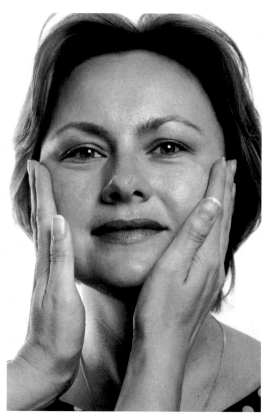

Prep your skin with a lightweight moisturiser (the air-con in offices can dry skin out). I would also recommend applying a serum primer to ensure stay-proof makeup all day if you tend to do lots of running around.

Apply a sheer foundation over areas of your skin that you would like to even out and conceal areas that need extra coverage with concealer – commonly around the nose, where most people have some redness.

Apply eye cream beneath your eyes along the highest point of your cheekbone to ensure that this area is well moisturised prior to applying corrector and concealer.

Apply under-eye corrector from the inner corner of your eye to the dark area beneath your eyes. Blend this towards the outer corner of your eyes where redness sometimes occurs. Apply your skin-toned concealer very lightly over the top of this and use your foundation brush to buff over the area and make it uniform.

Apply a peachy pink cream blusher to the apples of your cheeks and blend out towards the temples.

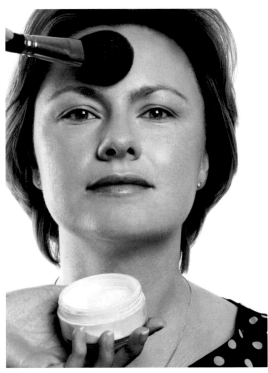

Press face powder over your face, particularly around the T-zone and over your cheeks, to set the cream blusher (ensuring it's light enough that you still get the glow of the cream blusher).

Sweep bronzer over the high points of your face, your forehead just below the hairline, your cheekbones, down the centre of your nose, your brow bone, your chin and your neck and décolletage (collar bone). Using a fluffy powder brush, blend from left to right in a sweeping motion, particularly across your forehead as this will move the product down the face in a gradual way to mimic the definition of a real tan.

Fill any sparse areas of your brows in lightly using a brow wax, felt tip, or pencil.

141

Apply a light, skin-toned eyeshadow all over your eyelid up to the socket line to even the colour out. A cream shadow also works well as a base here for long-lasting eyeshadow. Next, take a medium-toned eyeshadow and blend it all over the eyelid from the lower lash line up to the socket line.

Push gel eyeliner into your upper and lower lash line to create an illusion of thicker lashes without a hard solid line.

Pop mascara onto your upper and lower lashes, simply touching the wand to your lower lashes to give some colour without obvious product. Zigzag the wand at the root of your upper lashes for definition, leaving the ends fluttery with a small sweep of product.

Press a peachy pink lip colour into your lips and for extra definition, feather a lip liner over your lips.

143

A black-tie occasion

Paula is a primary school teacher and for this reason most of her days are spent in smart casual clothes and little to no makeup. We thought it would be fun to create a look suitable enough for school, but polished enough to wear to a corporate event or even a black-tie do! This is also a perfect look for customer-facing job roles where smart and beautiful presentation is key, like being an air hostess or the receptionist of a five-star hotel! It even looks great on a night out. Whatever occasion you choose to wear this, it will look gorgeously glamorous. If your eyes tend to drop at the outer corners and you still want to wear the kitten flick, trace it in when you are looking straight ahead into a mirror following your lower lash line (see page 67). Alternatively, this look can be worn without the kitten flick, and you can stop at the end of the lash line.

Skin

Step one
Apply foundation primer followed by a sheer coverage, buildable foundation to the centre of your face and blend outwards, continuing to build in areas that you feel require more coverage. Conceal blemishes with concealer and perfect under eyes with colour corrector and under-eye concealer – under-eye concealer may be enough alone but you can best judge that. Powder lightly to set the foundation and apply a very light veil of powder beneath the under eyes to prevent them from creasing.

Step two
Add warmth to your skin with a soft bronzer around the forehead, down the bridge of the nose, across the cheeks, on the chin and down the neck to ensure everything is blended well. Taking your fluffy powder brush, move from left to right down the face to blend all lines away and keep it flawless.

Eyes

Step one
Apply a skin-toned powder or cream eyeshadow all over the eyelid up to the brow bone. Apply highlighter to the inner corners of your eyes (the tear ducts).

Step two
Take a coloured eyeliner – I have used an emerald green here – and starting at the centre of the eyelid, trace the liner along the lash line tapering it out to the end of the eye, ending in a little kitten flick (see page 67). Continue the line in towards the inside corner of your eye, tapering it thinner as you go. (If you are applying it to someone else, ask the person to look down towards the floor at this point so that you can get neatly into the corner of the eye.

When eyes are closed it can cause transfer onto the lower lash line.) The thickest part of the eyeliner should be in the centre of the eyelid.

Step three
Curl lashes and apply three coats of gorgeous thick, black mascara.

Pretty natural peaches and cream

Amanda was 'mother of the bride' for one of my recent brides. She is a lovely, confident and smiley lady, with big sparkly chocolate brown eyes. I wanted to capture a polished look that would complement her pastel peach top and pearl necklace. I chose a peaches and cream look.

A hydrating, lightweight gel moisturiser was applied to Amanda's skin, followed by a beautiful gel foundation with a lovely dewy finish.

I then applied an apricot cream blush to the apples of her cheeks and dusted her skin with translucent powder.

I added a soft pop of peach to the apples of Amanda's cheeks and some bronzer to the high points of her face for a subtle sun-kissed glow. (Hairline, nose, cheeks, chin and neck.)

I swept a light pearl silver eyeshadow over Amanda's eyelids and slightly into the crease of her eyes so that when she opens and closes them they just catch the light. I then ran a black gel eyeliner along her upper lash line, into the roots and then slightly thicker for definition and to really open up her eyes. I kept the lower lash line bare to keep her eyes fresh and sparkly. Amanda's eyelashes were curled and then a couple of coats of black mascara were applied to her upper and lower lashes.

Brows were tidied ever so lightly and under-eye concealer applied lightly beneath the eyes with a soft fluffy brush.

Lastly, a nude peachy brown lip liner was applied to Amanda's lip line. I then sketched in her lips slightly and glossed them up with a clear lip-gloss.

Inner sparkle outwards

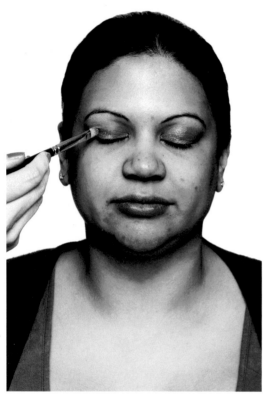 

Anjali was a bride of mine who I just adored working with. She literally radiates positivity and happiness. Every time she smiles her entire face lights up and her eyes sparkle. I wanted Anjali's makeup to really reflect this gentle, friendly, outgoing aspect of her personality. When she looked into the mirror she could see the beautiful, sparkly woman that we all see.

I used sparkle on Anjali's eyes, and so chose to do her eyes first so that I wouldn't have glitter dropping all over her base. Using a flat eyeshadow brush I first pressed primer onto her eyelids, followed by a gold glitter eyeshadow all over the lower eyelid.

I applied a dark sheeny brown to the socket line of Anjali's eyes and blended it down over the gold to just above the upper lash line to deepen the effect slightly. I left the lash line gold because with Anjali's hooded eyes I wanted the gold to still glimmer. I applied a bone-coloured eyeshadow beneath her brow bone to define them.

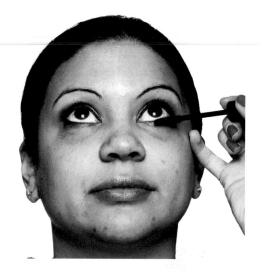

I lined Anjali's upper and lower lash line with a black gel liner. I then softened the lower lash line with a deep brown eyeshadow from the inner corner to the outer corner. I also lined the waterline of her eyes with black kohl eyeliner.

Anjali's eyelashes were curled and coated top and bottom in jet-black mascara.

I applied a sheer coverage foundation to Anjali's skin and used concealer for areas of blemishes to create a flawless finish.

I applied a yellow under-eye corrector to the under-eye area followed by a concealer. Using a fluffy eyeshadow brush I lightly set this area.

I powdered Anjali's face and then contoured her cheekbones, jawline, hairline and nose using a brown powder bronzer.

I applied a vibrant baby pink blush to the apples of Anjali's cheeks.

Eyebrows were tidied through with brow wax to give them a slightly fuller appearance.

Finally, a berry lipstick and a clear gloss were applied to her lips.

The dinner date

My vision of makeup for a dinner date is soft, feminine, classy and sophisticated. An ethereal look, warm and dreamy, that exudes a gentle, friendly personality. Opt for colours that look beautiful with soft candlelight: golds or soft silvers are a lovely option, or soft colours like purples. I love using eyeshadows that contain a fine shimmer that sparkles gently under candlelight. When I first met my husband I wasn't expecting to! I literally popped on some foundation, a little bit of blusher, some lipstick and a little bit of glitter eyeliner, which I used as an eyeshadow and finished with mascara. It was a really basic look, but I looked like me, which still to this day he says is what he loved. So many women worry about impressing men that they cake on lots of makeup, and whilst wearing lots of different looks is fun, any look from the smokiest of eyes to the most minimal no-makeup-makeup can be achieved without looking like you are plastered in products. Thin layers worked into the skin and built up in stages are how we achieve this.

Remember, on a date YOU are deciding if he is right for you, not whether you are right for him (and vice versa for him). The person worth investing in a relationship with will like you for all of you, not just your looks. I think the best look to go for on a dinner date is a polished version of you.

Step one
Apply foundation with a fibre-optic
foundation brush for a flawless airbrushed
finish. A foundation with a silk finish (matte
with a soft sheen) will look beautiful. It's not
overdewy and shiny, and it's also not too
matte and flat. Apply it all over your face
beginning at the centre and blending it out
towards the perimeter of your face,
including lightly over your eyelids and
beneath the eyes. Brighten lightly beneath
the eyes where any dark areas can be seen –
correct the colour first and then conceal!
(See page 43.)

Step two
Conceal any blemishes you would like to
deflect attention from with concealer.

Step three

Blend a soft cream blusher over the apples of your cheeks – dusty pinks and peaches are a lovely option. I chose bronze and apricot for Teena to complement her beautiful tan.

Step four

Powder the face gently with a translucent powder focusing mainly on the T-zone, or particularly shiny areas. It is always good to set cream blusher with powder to make it long-lasting.

Step five

Press a gold, silver or champagne eyeshadow with a fine shimmer or sparkle over your lower eyelid. I've chosen a warm gold for Teena. Take a mahogany brown eyeshadow or a soft grey and contour the socket line of your eyes to emphasise their shape. I have applied mahogany brown here.

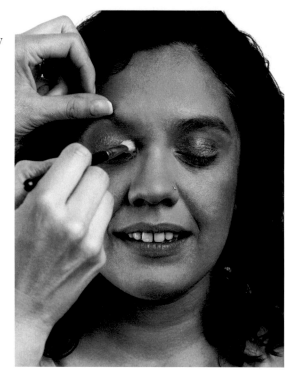

Step six
Line the upper lash line with dark brown eyeliner. Keep the lower lash line soft and run your mahogany brown eyeshadow along it.

Step seven
Curl your lashes and apply three coats of mascara for subtle drama. Flirty eyes are a must!

Step eight
Define your eyebrows with a soft shadow or brow wax.

Step nine
Apply a soft, red, glossy stain to your lips – confident and kissable!

155

A pretty hint of colour

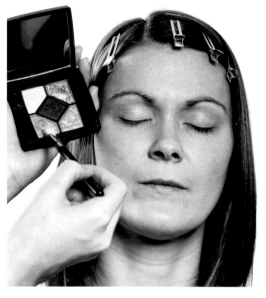

I began with Sam's eyes, sweeping a light eyeshadow all over her eyelids.

I then pressed a lilac eyeshadow over her eyelids and up into the crease (socket line) of her eyes.

I lined Sam's upper lash line using black gel eyeliner and a fine eyeliner brush.

A darker shade of purple was pressed into the outer corners of Sam's eyes in the shape of a triangle and I then used a fluffy eyeshadow brush to blend the edges into the rest of the eye makeup.

I then smudged the darker shade of purple over the eyeliner on the top lash line, and lined Sam's lower lash line with the dark shade of purple eyeshadow too. To add extra emphasis, black kohl eyeliner was applied to Sam's waterline.

Sam then curled her lashes, pumping them lightly approximately ten times on each eye, and I then applied black mascara to her eyelashes from root to the tip. (I always ask my clients if they prefer to curl their own.)

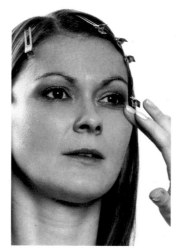

I wiped away any fall out from the eyeshadow beneath Sam's eyes and then began her base, using my fingertips to blend a sheer coverage gel foundation into her skin.

I brightened Sam's under-eye area with a yellow-based corrector pen, and used the same light-reflective pen beneath her eyebrows for a soft highlight.

Using a dry mascara wand, I swept Sam's eyebrows into place. I then used an angled eyebrow brush and brow wax to fill through them slightly for definition.

Bronzer was applied to Sam's cheeks, forehead, nose, chin and neck and blended seamlessly with a powder brush.

I applied a vibrant pink lipstick to Sam's lips very softly; I chose a bright colour that would make her lips appear slightly fuller. I feathered pink lip liner onto her lips to push the lip line slightly further out.

To finish the look, I popped a bright pink blusher onto the apples of the cheeks for a healthy, girly glow.

159

Simple summery makeup

I love this look – in the summer it looks beautiful against sun-kissed skin, during the winter it warms a pale complexion, and it suits all skin tones, hair colours and eye colours.

This is very much a skin-focused and dewy look, and prepping the skin with lovely moisturiser and foundation primer will give your complexion a beautiful, nourished appearance. When you apply foundation on top of this, it will look smooth and luxurious.

The next step is to conceal any blemishes or redness around the nose and brighten the under eyes. I have used a yellow corrector against Irene's tanned skin, followed by concealer.

Powder the T-zone of your face (forehead, nose and chin) and leave the cheeks powder-free for more of a glow.

Apply a fine shimmer or cream highlight to the tops of the cheekbones.

Apply bronzer to your cheeks, hairline, bridge of your nose, chin and neck. Blend well and then apply a pop of blusher to the apples of your cheeks for a healthy English rose complexion.

Press a skin-toned shimmer all over your eyelid, up to the crease (socket line), so that the sun can catch the sparkle of your eyes. Pop a small amount of shimmer on the inner corner of your eyes by the tear ducts so that when you open your eyes they look bright and awake.

Apply eyeliner to the top lash line, pressing it into the roots and keeping it very thin for subtle definition.

Apply mascara to your top and bottom lashes for wide-awake eyes to really enhance that sparkle.

Tidy through your brows softly.

Apply lip-gloss for a gentle, kissable shine.

163

Pretty colourful day makeup

Lisa has such a warm, friendly, happy and sweet personality; I felt that I really wanted to reflect this through her makeup. Lisa had a specific aim as she wanted to learn how to apply a fun and natural day look. Rather than just sticking to neutrals, she wanted to play around with some colour. Lisa has beautiful blue eyes, fair skin and brunette hair, so I chose a soft purple which complements all of these features. It also ties in very nicely with her striking turquoise nails, which are perfect for the summer.

Skin

Step one
Apply moisturiser to your skin, followed by a silk finish liquid foundation.

Step two
Apply a dusty pink cream blusher to the apples of your cheeks.

Step three
Conceal any areas that need further coverage.

Step four
Set your foundation and blusher with a sweep of translucent powder.

Step five
Bronze your cheeks, forehead, nose, chin and neck very slightly for soft warmth to the skin, and dust a small sweep of powder pearl finish blusher over the apples of the cheeks for a gentle glow.

Eyes

Step one

Apply eye primer to your eyelids.

Step two

Press a soft purple or pink eyeshadow over the lower eyelid. Choose cool-toned, blue-based pinks and purples; warm tones tend to have a lot of red-base to them, which can make eyes look as if they are sore, or bruised! Sweep the eyeshadow gently into the socket line so that it is just a haze of colour.

Step three

Line your upper lash line with black gel liner or black kohl pencil. Keep the line thin, running it along the root of your lashes. Take a vibrant iridescent purple eyeshadow and press it over the eyeliner with a fine brush. Softly line your lower lash line with the same purple eyeshadow. Apply mascara to your upper and lower lashes.

Step four

Tidy your eyebrows. Lisa's eyebrows start just slightly short – a common mistake because makeup tutors used to teach to use the inner corner of the eye (the tear duct) as a guide when shaping your eyebrows, when in fact the bridge of the nose in line with the centre of your nostril is the correct guide. To give Lisa's eyebrows more length I softened the start of them with a brow wax definer. Another good option would be to use a felt-tip brow pen to create individual hairs – this is particularly useful if the brows stop too short as it keeps them looking natural.

Lips

One of Lisa's main concerns was not being able to find a lip shade that suits her. I explained that by choosing a shade close to her natural lip colour (you can see this by holding the colour next to your lips, or by applying it to your fingertip where the skin is closest in colour to that of your lips) she would find the most flattering colour for her complexion. Lisa's natural lip colour falls in between a pink and a red, so I chose a lipstick shade with that same colour. Lisa suits both cool and warm tones, which again this lipstick has.

CHAPTER 10

Makeup in Minutes

Makeup on the move

There are those hectic mornings when we rush out of the house thinking, 'I'll do my makeup on the way to work', but the trick is managing to apply it nicely when you're travelling along on a bumpy train, a bus or in the car! This section was inspired by a young lady sitting next to me applying perfect eyeliner and mascara on the Tube. I was so inspired, I turned to her and said, 'That is very impressive'. She giggled and said, 'Thank you', a little taken aback that someone had actually spoken a word to another person on the Tube! If you live in London, you'll be all too familiar with the silence as everyone has their heads buried in their iPhones.

I have practised applying makeup whilst travelling on all forms of transport to ensure it works! Use your fingers for the entire makeover: it's fast and accurate because you have so much control with your hands.

Brushes can slip, slide and smudge – from personal experience I can guarantee a bump and a brush in the eye is very painful and a definite mess.

Carry a compact mirror in your handbag, along with a makeup wipe or two! Apply your foundation using small circular motions of the fingertips, starting from your nose and working out towards your cheeks, up onto your forehead and down over your chin. Focusing the coverage on the centre of your face gives the quickest, most natural look. If you have blemishes, use your fingertip to pat over them with concealer.

Using your fingertip, swipe some colour or sparkle over your eyelid.

It takes time to master the art of using eyeliner on the Tube. Your best bet is to wait until you get to work, but if you really can't live without it, use a wax pencil that's easy to smudge, move or wipe away if you make a mistake. Alternatively, use your finger to press a dark, cream eyeshadow into the root of your eyelashes to give the illusion of eye-liner.

Apply your mascara very carefully! If you know you'll make a mess, switch to clear mascara just for those days.

Use your lipstick as a blush and blend it into the apples of your cheeks, use the same lip colour on your lips.

If you prefer to use powder, pop a bronze and blush compact into your handbag. After you've done your foundation sweep on some powder, then pop some bronzer onto the high points of your face (bridge of your nose, forehead, tops of cheekbones and chin). Blend this seamlessly and sweep the brush over your neck so that it doesn't appear disconnected in colour. Finish with a dusting of blusher on your cheekbones and blend towards the apples of your cheeks.

The bold and the bright lip

Turn a simple day look into a seductive evening-out look by changing the lip colour! I love how versatile one face can be.

The day look

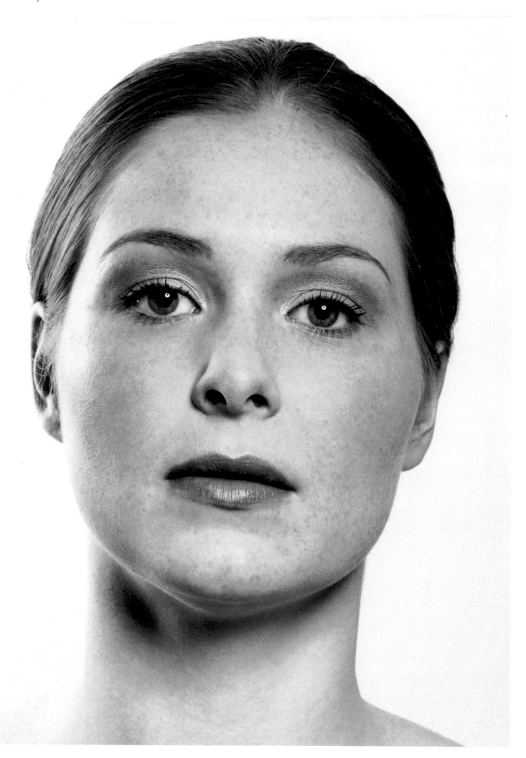

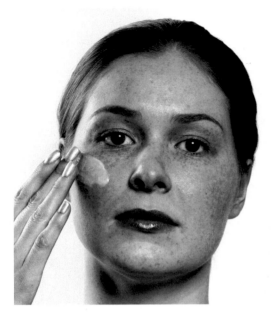

Prep your skin with moisturiser and/or foundation primer to create a smooth, long-lasting base for the rest of your makeup.

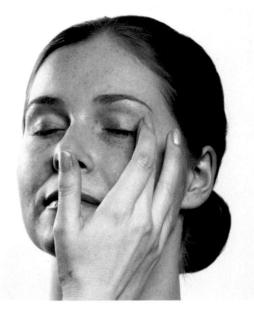

Apply eye cream under your eyes to prep them for concealer (this prevents the concealer becoming caked beneath your eyes).

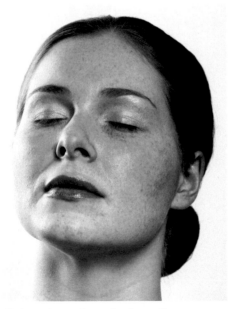

Press a light coloured eyeshadow all over your eyelids. In this case I have applied the shade up to the brow bone, making the eyes my main focus because of the high shimmer level.

Apply a bronze eyeshadow into the crease of your eyes and blend it slightly down onto your eyelids.

Push gel eyeliner into the roots of your lashes to create natural definition of the eyes. Follow this with mascara on your top and bottom lashes.

Blend a sheer foundation into your skin to give a subtle glow. I have used a very sheer gel formula on model Emily so that we can see her beautiful freckles. Try to avoid covering freckles because it always looks unnatural, ashy and chalky, plus freckles are so pretty and they add a certain warmth to a complexion.

Use a fine concealer brush to pinpoint concealer over the top of blemishes. Use just the tip of the bristles incredibly lightly.

Pat an under-eye corrector pen beneath the eyes, followed by a small touch of concealer.

Blend a cream blusher into the apples of your cheeks – the warmth of your fingertips works best.

Highlight the top of your cheekbones with a cream highlighter.

Apply a vibrant lip colour softly to the lips so that you see just a hint of that colour. Press the same lipstick shade just over the apples of your cheeks to make the complexion pop.

Define your brows with a touch of brow wax and a small angled brush.

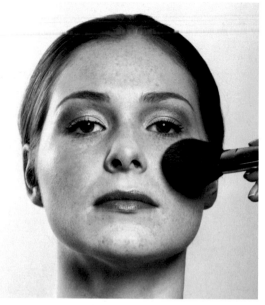

Set the makeup and remove excess shine with a sweep of translucent powder.

The vibrant lip

Emily's hair was waved to create a classic, sleek style and I applied a rich, vibrant orange lipstick to her lips. This complements her red hair and bronzed eye makeup.

The evening look

We shook out the waves in Emily's hair to give it more movement and I applied a deep, dark berry lipstick. Fair-skinned girls (particularly redheads) often think that they could not pull off vibrant or dark colours, and so I wanted to show you that you can, and it can look hot! Again, the neutral mix of warm and cool within this lipstick complements her hair colour, skin tone and eye colour perfectly.

The red lip

Confidence in a Tube

Did you know that a man's heart rate speeds up when he looks at red lipstick? It's like the adrenalin rush of a fast red car!

The red lip is a simple and fast way of creating a classy, stunning look. One of the nicest ways to wear it is against neutral, glowing skin and nude eyes, so that the lips become the statement feature. It is a look that enhances your confidence; it looks powerful and elegant and is perfect for interviews, dinners, parties, and day-to-day life! Red lipstick has always been my interview thing, – it's like putting on my confidence suit. I was adamant as a teenager that it was my red lipstick that got me the job every time.

Choosing the red that complements you most is something that a lot of women have trouble with. The simplest way is to pop it onto your fingertip and hold it against your lips. Smile, and if your teeth look white and your complexion glows next to the colour you have the right shade. It is important that the shade doesn't appear stark next to your skin, thus making you look washed out; it should complement your skin tone. Generally, fair skin tones look lovely in blue-based reds (cool tones), whilst warm skin tones look fabulous in orange-based reds (warm tones).

Prep your lips with a balm first so that they are soft and supple – red really clings to dry skin, and you want them to look seductive and smooth. Take a tissue and blot away excess lip balm. Using feather-like strokes, line your lips with a lip liner, filling them in slightly as you go so that there is no hard line. A similar colour to the colour of the lipstick you will be using is good but if you don't have that, use a nude lip liner instead. This helps to make the lipstick long-lasting and also prevents the product creeping onto the skin around your mouth. Use a lip brush for precision, and press the lipstick into your lips. Blot again with a tissue and apply the last coat of lipstick, following your lip line carefully. At this point you can either leave it there, apply a gloss on top for shine, a lip balm on top for soft sheen, or for a matte lip, press loose powder gently over them. My personal favourite is a red lip with a sheen – healthy, classy and not too messy!

Colourful smoky eyes

Smoky eyes are traditionally thought of as black, however you can in fact use absolutely any colour in the spectrum. These neon smoky eyes are a perfect look for summer and make a fun statement.

Prime your eyes with eye primer or concealer, sweep a skin-toned eyeshadow all over the eyelid into the socket line, then press a vibrant colour up to the socket line. Take your fluffy brush and blend the colour through the socket line, back and forth, so that the colour gradually fades towards your eyebrows.

Tidy your brows, apply a pop of blusher onto your cheeks, and finally use a sheer tinted lip balm similar to that of your own natural lip colour.

Beach chic

This look has been created for two reasons. Firstly, it's for those days when you are at the beach and want an effortlessly sexy, long-lasting makeup, and secondly, it's for when you just want to look like you are on holiday, rain or shine! At this present moment the sun is beaming down on my laptop as I sit outside in a summer dress soaking up the rays of the English sun. This is one of those rare moments when England feels the sun's heat ... yes, it does exist! We all go racing out to catch it before it disappears again. So, I feel perfectly prepped to write this section on beach-ready makeup!

Long-lasting waterproof makeup is the key to this look; it is sexy in an undone manner. Hair is tousled, skin is bronzed and cheeks are flushed. The sun gives you that glow, and that incredibly healthy-looking shine to your skin. There is a hint of colour or shimmer upon your eyelids that embraces the fun colours of the season. Lips look healthy, soft and kissable.

Apply sunscreen to your face and neck, and lip balm to your lips before you get started on makeup.

179

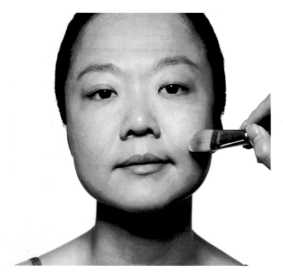

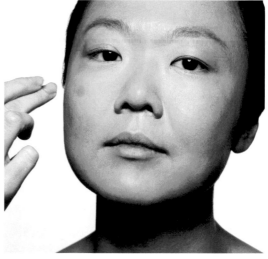

Apply oil based, sheer coverage waterproof foundation to your face, focusing mainly on the T-zone and cheeks. Blend the product sparsely across the rest of your face being careful to blend it invisibly on the jawline. Brighten the under-eye area with corrector and concealer.

Blend a waterproof pink blusher onto the top of your cheekbones, your hair line, nose, chin and shoulders. Set the skin with face powder. Don't worry if it looks too bright at the moment!

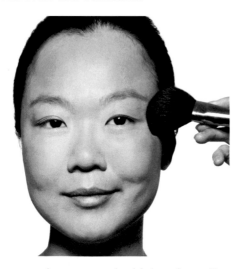

Apply matte bronzer to the high points of the face that you applied the blusher to. Use a big powder brush and sweeping motions to blend any visible lines away. Apply a shimmer highlighter to your cheeks.

Using your fingertip, swipe a long-lasting cream eyeshadow (I have chosen turquoise) across your lower eyelid and blend it gently into the socket line (all with your fingertips unless you want to use an eyeshadow brush). I have also applied a gold eyeliner to the waterline of Bridget's lower lash line to catch the glimmer of the sun – it looks beautiful next to her tanned skin.

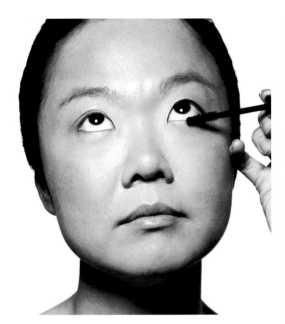

Apply waterproof mascara to your top and bottom lashes.

Press a tinted lip balm, or a creamy lipstick, onto your lips – peach or coral complements a tan perfectly.

Let your hair down and scrunch it with beach spray (texturising spray) for that 'at the beach' natural wave.

181

Simple makeup for work

Diane works in healthcare. It's important to remember that taking care of yourself is really important when you are taking care of other people. A bright lippie is a great way to feel amazing in zero time.

Step one
Moisturise your skin and buff a lightweight, long-lasting, hydrating foundation into your skin.

Step two
Conceal any areas that you feel need extra coverage with a matte concealer.

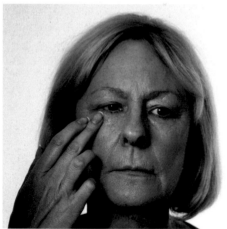

Step three
Apply a hydrating eye gel beneath the eyes to prepare them for under-eye concealer. Keeping this area well moisturised will help to prevent the makeup creasing or becoming cakey.

Step four
Conceal any under-eye darkness with concealer of your choice.

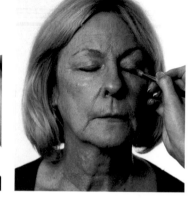

Step five
Apply a vibrant blusher to the apples of your cheeks and blend away towards the temples. The colour should make the skin pop with radiance.

Step six
Run a teal eyeshadow or eyeliner along your lower lash line. Apply a purple eyeshadow or eyeliner to the upper lash line. Turn your eyeshadow into an eyeliner by applying it with a damp eyeliner brush (water or eyeshadow transformer liquid can be used, eyeshadow transformer liquid has great staying power).

Step nine
Red lipstick is a great, professional colour full of confidence and can be worn softly for a subtle glow. Press the lipstick gently into your lips following the lip shape. Apply a lip-gloss or balm over the top to keep lips looking and feeling well nourished.

Step seven
Enhance eyebrows by running a brow wax gently through the hair following your natural shape.

Step eight
Apply mascara to your top and bottom lashes.

CHAPTER 11

Considering Semi-Permanent Makeup

I have included this next chapter due to popular demand and my own love of the procedure. Semi-permanent makeup is fantastic for plumping thinning lips and thickening sparse brows and lashes. It miraculously widens eyes and can even help to reduce the appearance of fine lines. Read on to find out more …

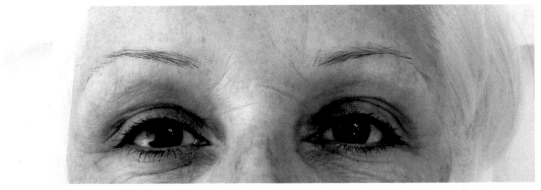

I first came across semi-permanent makeup when I met talented semi-permanent makeup artist Helen Porter. Strolling through Canterbury town one sunny afternoon, I wandered past the building site that was to be Helen's new salon 'Evolution Skin Studios', jointly created with cosmetic surgeon John Davison – I wandered in to meet Helen and chat about the plans for the new salon, which is now open and a big success. Helen is a master trainer in the art of semi-permanent makeup and medical tattooing. Working alongside dermatologists and surgeons, she has pushed the boundaries for scar camouflage and has travelled to America and various venues throughout the UK to lecture on this subject. The procedure is used throughout the world, both cosmetically and medically.

I have watched Helen apply semi-permanent eyeliner, eyebrows and lip liner and the results were truly amazing. The new level of confidence that it brings to people is indescribable. I regularly work with cancer patients and terminally ill patients, using makeup therapy with regular makeup products – not only do patients have to deal with the journey of fighting their illness, but with physical appearance changes too, which can be somewhat emotionally challenging. Together we find solutions to combat their concerns – for example, a simple semi-permanent felt-tip eyebrow pen could be used to mimic the appearance of individual hair forming the shape and definition of an eyebrow. Semi-permanent makeup works in the same way, but the results last a lot longer! Not only does semi-permanent makeup work miracles in the medical world, but it can also be used by those who are concerned about ageing. Semi-permanent makeup can be used to reduce the appearance of fine lines and wrinkles, in the same way as it can reduce the appearance of scars, whether acne scars or severe bodily or facial scarring. I caught up with Helen over coffee to find out more about the subject …

What is semi-permanent makeup?

Semi-permanent makeup, also known as SPMU, is makeup that is applied beneath the top layers of the skin so that it stays on day after day; no smudges nor any need to reapply throughout the day.

The idea of SPMU is to naturally enhance the facial features in a soft and subtle way. It can refresh tired-looking eyes, add the appearance of volume to lashes, correct uneven and sparse brows and it can redefine lip shape, creating definition and giving the illusion of fuller, plumper lips using a soft lip line. Applying a full lip colour can mimic the beautiful rose hue to your lips that you have when you wake in the morning – that healthy glow can stay day after day, hour after hour.

Like all makeup, SPMU should flatter the features, and not overpower them. Less is always best.

Could you summarise the benefits of SPMU for our readers?

Yes, of course:

- Beautiful enhancement of facial features
- No smudges
- No re-applying throughout the day
- Time saved applying makeup every day
- You can wake up perfectly made-up, morning after morning
- You can swim to your heart's content and your makeup will never disappear – or run down your face!

What looks can be achieved with SPMU?

This procedure is so diverse. I'll run through what can be achieved, feature by feature:

Your eyebrows

Block, powdered or 3D hair stroke

Block brows will give you the same result as applying an eyebrow pencil; it will be very defined and solid, ideal if you love a strong or dominant brow.

The 3D hair stroke will look as close to a natural brow as you can get. Individual strokes are applied to give the illusion of real hair – this is great for people who would like a little more definition to their brow without it looking like makeup. This technique is great for people with very sparse or no brow hair at all.

The powdered technique is somewhere between block and 3D hair stoke. It is done by applying the cosmetic hairs more densely than with the 3D hair stroke, so that you gain the appearance of a more solid brow but minus the solid edges.

Your Eyes

Lash Enhancement is done by applying small dots between each lash to give the appearance of more lashes, which is good for people who never wear makeup and may be a little nervous about what the outcome may look like. It is a great technique for very sparse lashes.

Fine Liner is created by applying a very fine line through the lashes to give the appearance of a thicker set of lashes. Most people like to have a fine line through the bottom lashes but end up making the top lashes thicker on a second visit.

Medium Liner is the most popular effect; it is a lovely technique that gives the appearance of luscious thick lashes on the top and bottom lid, which gives definition and frames the eyes, making them the focal point of the face.

Latino Liner is a brilliant option for people who wear thick eyeliner every day and like to wear heavier eye makeup. Generally the top liner is applied finely at the inner part of the eye, thickening out to an elongated flick at the outer corner. What you must take into consideration with this look is that it's normally done with black pigment, and black can last several years within the skin (sometimes indefinitely). You will have this look every day, morning and night, and it is virtually impossible to remove if you decide you no longer like the heavy look. So think long and hard before committing to this style.

Your lips

Lip Liner can be applied in two different ways – a fine line can be applied to the border of the lips to give them a crisp edge – framing, emphasising and giving volume – or alternatively, a thicker line can be applied to give a softer definition to the lip.

Lip Blush is beautiful for people who want the definition of a lip liner without looking like they only have a line. A soft blush of colour can be applied to blend the outline into the natural colour of the lip; this is perfect for natural enhancement.

Full Lips are often advised for people who want their lips to be permanently made-up. Colours can be natural or more vibrant depending on the look that you desire. The shape can be enhanced and a solid colour will be applied. All you need from here to complement your new lips perfectly is a subtle layer of lip-gloss and you'll never have the need to reapply lippy again. However, if you do decide you need to change the colour to suit an outfit you can apply regular lipstick over the top as you would normally.

How is semi-permanent makeup applied?

Using a digital hand-held machine, very fine needles gently break the surface of the skin allowing the implantation of hypoallergenic pigments into the dermal layer. This pigment will, after a healing process, stay in the skin for a number of years, breaking down and fading with time, dependant on the client's age and skin type, and exposure to the sun.

How long does the treatment generally last?

It is impossible to put a timescale on the expected life span of SPMU. As a guide most specialists recommend returning once a year to have something that is called a colour boost (top up/colour refresh). During this session the specialist may decide to apply more pigment into the skin to ensure that the shape holds for another year, or the client may decide to alter the colour to a lighter or darker shade and possibly even thicken the appearance. Treatment is not always needed at this point but it's good to go for a check-up just to be sure. As a general rule, the darker the colour, the longer it should last.

What are the guidelines for having the procedure done?

You must be over eighteen to have this procedure due to the Tattooing of Minors Act 1969. There are a few medical conditions and/or medications that may prevent you having the procedure done; if you suffer from any medical illness it is always a good idea to check with your specialist before booking the treatment. It will not necessarily mean you can never have treatment but there may be certain things that you can do prior to the treatment to ensure that your health is never jeopardised.

What things should you take into consideration once you have had the treatment done?

Due to the necessary abrasion to the skin, slight swelling or redness may occur immediately after the procedure. This should subside over the next couple of hours, however your eyes may stay puffy for a few days if you have sensitive eyes. The colour may look a little intense for the first three to seven days, during which time the skin will dry slightly and shed, revealing softer colour beneath.

After four weeks you should go back for a check-up. In this appointment you can decide if you would like to go any thicker or darker, and gaps can be filled in and you can make small adjustments.

There are no guarantees as to how long SPMU will last – it could be months or even several years, which is why it's never advised to have fashion makeup, due to the fact that a particular fashion trend may fade long before the makeup does.

How much does it cost and what maintenance is needed?

Depending on the area that you live in prices can vary quite dramatically. Although you want to get the most out of your money, cost should never be the deciding factor on which semi-permanent makeup artist you choose to carry out the procedure. It is always a good idea to phone a few different salons to get an idea of the prices in your area.

So, how do we find the right specialist?

This is the most important question that you should ask yourself before embarking on such a procedure. You must be confident that the person you choose is on your wavelength. Many of us have had our makeup done by someone at some stage in our lives and disliked it, rubbing it off as soon as we can. This may not be because the makeup was applied poorly but that it was just not what you personally like for yourself. This is the same with SPMU; some specialists are very versatile and can adapt to individuals, but some have a very strong style, so it is essential that you look through their portfolios to see examples of their work prior to committing to the treatment.

What health and safety regulations should we seek out?

This procedure is technically classed as tattooing because a small needle is used to penetrate the skin. So all the hygiene rules that apply to tattoos apply to SPMU.

What questions should we ask the specialist?
You should be able to see a licence supplied by the council to show the studio has been approved.

Equipment – The equipment must be council approved, all needles should be disposable and the pack should be opened in front of you. Some of the old machines do not comply with current regulations as their individual parts cannot be sterilized and cross contamination can occur, so make sure you ask which machine is being used – you can contact your local council or do a Google search to find out if it has been approved as safe. The hand piece, machine and trolley should be covered in protective plastic that must be disposed of after use. You should never be asked to keep hold of your needle and ink cap as bacteria will grow and cause a potential infection when used again. There should be protective paper on the couch that you lie on.

You should have access to see a certificate of qualification, a local licence that allows the technician you are seeing to practice cosmetic tattooing on the premises and current insurance documents.

Closing the interview: Helen, thank you for taking the time to answer these questions for our readers. This procedure enhances lives all over the globe and I hope that it will be of great help to anyone who may be considering the treatment, or who didn't know it was available until reading this.

Semi-permanent makeup artist Helen Porter.

CHAPTER 12

Makeup & Glasses

I wanted to include this section for those of you who wear glasses. A friend of mine recently asked me for advice on how to apply eyeliner whilst wearing glasses. It takes some practice but it is possible to apply it from above or below the glasses if you adjust the angle of them. See page 68 for detailed instructions.

Contrary to popular belief, you do not need to apply heavy eye makeup to make it visible beneath glasses. If you don't like to wear a lot of makeup, simply applying eyeliner can give enough definition to compensate for the frame. Mannetta tends not to wear makeup very often, so I chose to take this approach with her look. The great thing about eyeliner is that you can use all sorts of different colours to change your look and mood.

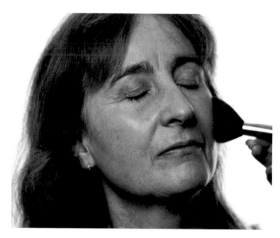

Step one:

I applied moisturiser, foundation and under-eye concealer to Mannetta's skin. I then used a fuchsia pink lipstick as a cream blusher. I popped it onto the apples of her cheeks and blended it out over her cheek-bones towards the temples.

Step two:

Mannetta's skin was powdered lightly and then a little baby pink powder blusher was swept over the apples of her cheeks for an extra-healthy glow.

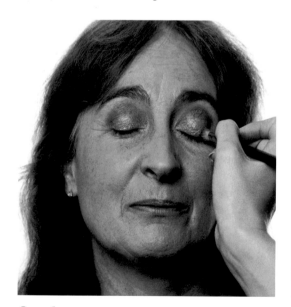

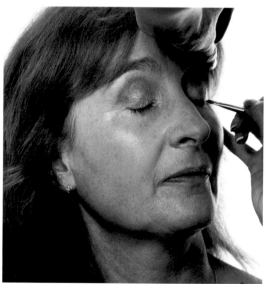

Step three:

I pressed a metallic gold eyeshadow over Mannetta's eyelids and then a mahogany eyeshadow through the socket line and slightly onto the outer corner of the eyelids.

Step four:

Dark brown gel eyeliner was pressed along the upper lash line to really lift and open the eyes. The lower lash line was kept bare to keep the eyes looking fresh.

Step five:
Black mascara was applied to Mannetta's
top and bottom lashes, building upon each
layer whilst still wet to prevent spider
lashes (clogging together).

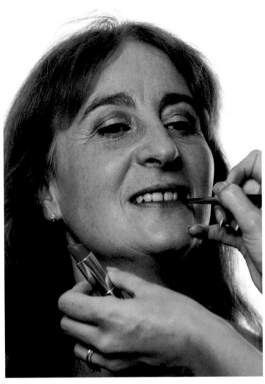

Step seven:
Lastly, I tidied Mannetta's eyebrows with
brow wax to frame her face alongside
her glasses.

Step six:
I love Mannetta in her pink sweater, and so
used a fuchsia pink lipstick to complement
the outfit and give her complexion a real
glow. I enjoy showing women that they can
wear these vivid, neon hues and look
amazing in them at absolutely any age!
Sometimes the older a person, the more
amazing they look in vivid colours because
as we age, our skin can become sallow in
tone. Vivid colours can really lift sallow
skin, making it appear healthy and
youthful.

CHAPTER 13

Before & After Enhanced Beauty

Claire has beautiful bright blue eyes, warm peach skin and blonde hair, so I decided that apricots would really enhance her colouring. I buffed foundation into Claire's skin and brightened the under-eye area. I applied an apricot eyeshadow all over her eyelids and used a fluffy eyeshadow brush to blend it into the socket line. Then I popped a creamy skin-toned eyeshadow beneath her eyebrows to highlight the area slightly. To enhance the appearance of Claire's eyelashes I wiggled a mascara wand at the root of her upper eyelashes. I touched the lower eyelashes lightly with the mascara wand to define the lashes softly whilst keeping the under-eye area light. Claire's eyebrows were defined lightly with a blonde eyebrow wax.

I warmed the skin with an apricot blusher over the cheekbones towards the outer perimeter of the face. A glossy peach lipstick gave Claire's look a really pretty, natural finish.

Caroline is such a gorgeous woman. She is one of the warmest and friendliest people I have worked with. She has always kept her look natural and pretty, and I wanted to portray this through her makeup. I used minimal makeup to enhance her features and create a simple, beautiful look.

I applied a small amount of foundation to Caroline's skin. She has a very clear, even skin tone naturally, so I used foundation purely to give it a radiant lift. I applied the same foundation over her eyelids to keep the entire face smooth and clear. I then used a vibrant berry pink lipstick on the apples of Caroline's cheeks and used my fingertips to blend the product over her cheekbones. I applied mascara to Caroline's upper lash line, tidied her eyebrows with brow wax and applied the same berry pink lipstick to her lips.

Samantha is a great photographer friend of mine. She has such a vibrant and fun personality, as sparkly as the sparkle of her chocolate brown eyes! I applied a cream finish, nourishing foundation to Samantha's skin, dusted her face lightly with face powder and then applied a neutral peach blusher to her cheekbones. I swept a bronze eyeshadow all over her eyelids and into the crease of her eyelids. Because Samantha has hooded eyelids I extended the eyeshadow beyond the crease and winged it out ever so slightly at the outer corner of the eyes. It is really important to use your lower lash line for an angle guide, so that you pull the eyeshadow upwards in the right direction and give the illusion of lifting the eyes. I applied soft brown eyeliner to the upper and lower lash line, followed by black mascara top and bottom. To finish, I swept brow mousse through Samantha's eyebrows and popped a pink lipstick onto her lips.

Georgia has beautiful features – crystal eyes and really full lips, and she looks totally glamorous all made up. When we shot this image, Georgia had just come back from a sunny holiday, and as we know all too well the tan on our face tends to fade pretty quickly because we are so often cleansing, applying makeup and cleansing again. So here is what to do in that situation: I applied a foundation roughly two shades darker to Georgia's face, matching the colour exactly to her chest and also blending it down on to her neck. (You can mix your foundation for the perfect shade, see page 40.)

I lightly powdered her skin and then applied a peony pink blusher to her cheekbones, blending it up and out towards the temples. I chose gold and bronze eyeshadow to complement Georgia's eye colour; I swept the gold eyeshadow over her lower eyelids and into the inner corner of the eyes to add a sparkle. The bronze eyeshadow was swept into the socket line. I then swept the same bronze eyeshadow along the lower lash line. Georgia is wearing individual false lashes, which she had put on for her holiday, so I applied mascara to the tips of these, and then mascara to her lower lashes. I swept a blonde brow wax through Georgia's eyebrows and finished the look with fuchsia pink lipstick and a lip-gloss to really enhance the fullness of her lips.

200

Lauren has such a cute look, so I felt a girl next-door makeup look would be perfect for her. I applied a gel foundation to Lauren's skin and popped a dusty pink blusher onto the apples of her cheeks. I swept a light bronze eyeshadow all over her eyelids and into the socket line. I then swept the same bronze eyeshadow along the lower lash line. I applied mascara to the top and bottom lashes, focusing most of the product at the root of the upper lashes. I tidied Lauren's eyebrows and applied a dusty pink lipstick to her lips for a pretty, girlie finish.

Paula is one of my beautiful best friends. She tends to wear her look pretty natural, unless I pull her in for a makeup shoot and play around with colour. I was inspired by a beachy, smudged eyeliner look I'd seen on my last trip to Australia for this look. We applied a little bit of fake tan to Paula's body, and a foundation in a shade to match her body to give her an overall summer glow. Paula is one of those lucky girls who literally only has to blink at the sun and she has this gorgeous olive tan! So, I wanted to play on that. I contoured Paula's cheeks slightly and then applied bronzer to the outer perimeter of her face. A light, skin-toned eyeshadow was swept over her eyelids and the bronzer was swept through the socket line for definition. I applied eyeliner to the upper lash line and then smudged the same black kohl eyeliner along the lower lash line. Mascara was applied to Paula's long eyelashes top and bottom, eyebrows were tidied and a red brick lipstick pressed into her lips for a soft and sexy appeal.

Paula's second look was achieved by blending a navy blue eyeshadow through the socket line. A pink blusher was applied to the apples of her cheeks, and a berry pink lipstick replaced the red brick lipstick. The overall feel of this look is cool and pretty.

Emma has a gorgeous warm hair colour which really emphasises her hazel green eyes. I chose an eyeshadow with the same warm undertone and teamed that with a lighter, gold eyeshadow. I swept the bronze eyeshadow through the socket line and left the lower lash line bare for a really fresh look. I applied mascara densely to the upper lash line, and lightly touched the lower lashes. An apricot blusher was swept over Emma's cheeks and an apricot lipstick finished this autumnal look.

207

Colour is beautiful, no matter what age you are. Rather than opting for a neutral look for Sally, I wanted to experiment with something youthful and fun. I chose gold eyeshadow on the lower eyelid, and purple eye shadow through the socket line to make her blue eye colour pop and lined her upper lash line with black gel liner, lifting the eyes and giving the colour extra definition. Peach blusher warmed Sally's fair complexion and a vibrant hue of red pink lipstick gave her lips a fuller appearance whilst keeping the overall look youthful and radiant.

CREDITS

Models

Bethany Rose Whittle – page ii

Emily Latham – pages viii, 8, 14, 53, 66, 74, 82, 94, 95, 169–175

Kate McIntyre – front cover, pages viii, 97

Anna Williamson – page 68

Claire – pages viii, 92, 98

Jane Newton – pages viii, 99

Pamela Nagappa – pages viii, 100, 101

Anjali Howard – pages 101, 148–151

Claire O'Connor – pages viii, 15, 90, 102, 103

Claire Tabony – pages 90, 194, 195

Lauren Tabony – pages 90, 202, 203

Irene Marco – pages 3, 6, 9, 16–20, 30, 33, 38, 39, 42, 51, 54, 67, 69, 73, 74, 76, 77, 80, 82, 85–89, 94, 160–163, 176, 177

Lucie Vigar – pages 8, 53, 108, 113–119

Bridget Lee – pages 9, 19, 20, 26, 48, 49, 62–65, 137, 179–181

Paula Brown – pages 11, 26, 27, 58, 60, 104–107, 145, 204–206

Marija Hume – pages 12, 14, 21, 40, 43, 47, 138–143,

Florence West – page 136

Minnie Rahman – page 13

Roshni Patel – page 41

Chelsea Nkala – page 40

Sarah de Mattos – page 127

Sally Rumbol – pages 208, 209

Georgia Ann Peck – pages 200, 201

Holly Jones and Natalie Shirlaw – closing collage

Teena Chowdhury – pages 152–155

Dinah Godfree – page 91

Mannetta Leigh-Ferguson – pages 191–193

Lynn Barwick – pages 122–125

Diane Bernier – pages 182–184

Sam Franklyn – pages 156–159

Gemma Robinson and Savannah Stephenson – pages 128–135

Holly Lumsden – closing collage

Caroline Sole – pages 32, 196, 197

Arti Danes – page 167

Toma – Nevs Models – pages 25, 61

Lisa McQuirns – pages 164–166

Samantha Jones – pages 198, 199

Tiffany Gledhill – page 24

Thandie – page 29

Kate Errington – pages 59, 178

Pink lipstick shot – page 79

Vicki Lord – page 91

Christine Braithwaite – pages 119–121

Amanda – page 147

Helen Porter – page 190

Emma Denning – page 207

Natalie Eacersall – closing collage

Laura – page 79

Natalie Georgiou – closing collage

Photographers

Jessica De Mattos – www.jessicademattos.com – pages viii, 3, 6–12, 14, 16–21, 26, 27, 30, 33–40, 42, 43, 47–58, 62–67, 69–77, 80–89, 91, 94, 95, 99–101, 104–166, 169–177, 179–184, 191–193

Richard Grebby – www.richardgrebby.co.uk – front cover, pages viii, 15, 32, 40 (second image), 41, 90, 92, 97, 98, 102, 103, 194–209

Ben Anker Photography – www.benankerphotography.co.uk – page 29

John Burgess – www.waterhamstudios.co.uk – folio brush image, pages i, ii, 4, 7 (second image), 8 (first and second brush images), 9 (fourth image), 13, 22, 59, 60, 79, 136, 178

Samantha Jones – www.samanthajonesphotography.co.uk – page 24

Matt Bristow – www.rubberduckdoes.com – page 56, 87

Darren Brade Photography – www.darrenbrade.com – page 68

Lotte Simons – www.lottesimons.com – closing collage (model Natalie Eacersall)

Hair Stylists

Semone Hairstylist

Vicki Lord Session Stylist – www.vickilord.co.uk

Natalie Shirlaw – www.shirlawsanctuary.com

Denim Magazine (Aug 2012) – pages 61, 167

Photographer – Will Sterling

Stylists – Romero Bryan, Sophia Jolly, Purplepeppa

Splinterz Hair Salon

Helen Porter – www.evolutionskinstudios.com – page 190

INDEX